ON THE
RIGHT TRACK

ON THE
RIGHT TRACK

FROM OLYMPIC DOWNFALL TO FINDING FORGIVENESS AND THE STRENGTH TO OVERCOME AND SUCCEED

MARION JONES

HOWARD BOOKS
A DIVISION OF SIMON & SCHUSTER, INC.

New York • Nashville • London • Toronto • Sydney

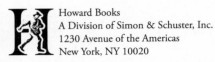

Howard Books
A Division of Simon & Schuster, Inc.
1230 Avenue of the Americas
New York, NY 10020

First Howard Books hardcover edition October 2010

HOWARD and colophon are trademarks of Simon & Schuster, Inc.

For information about special discounts for bulk purchases, please contact Simon & Schuster Special Sales at 1-866-506-1949 or business@simonandschuster.com.

The Simon & Schuster Speakers Bureau can bring authors to your live event. For more information or to book an event, contact the Simon & Schuster Speakers Bureau at 1-866-248-3049 or visit our website at www.simonspeakers.com.

Designed by Stephanie D. Walker

Manufactured in the United States of America

10   9   8   7   6   5   4   3   2   1

Library of Congress Cataloging-in-Publication Data
Jones, Marion
    On the right track : from Olympic downfall to finding forgiveness and the strength to overcome and succeed / Marion Jones ; with Maggie Greenwood-Robinson.
    p.   cm.
    1. Jones, Marion, 1975–   2. Runners (Sports)—United States—Biography.   3. Women runners—United States—Biography.   I. Greenwood-Robinson, Maggie.   II. Title.
    GV1061.15 J67A3 2010
    796.420922—dc22
    [B]   2010028584

ISBN 978-1-4516-1082-6
ISBN 978-1-4516-1083-3 (ebook)

To Oba, Monty, Amir, and Eva-Marie,
the loves of my life

ACKNOWLEDGMENTS

With very special thanks to Oba, Mom, Albert, Uncle Godwin, Christa, Hilda, Alvin, Rich, Hill, Henry D., Joe B., Howard, Sue, Melissa J., Tiffany, Henry M., Pastor Rob and Shoreline Christian Church, Maggie, Jan, Nena, the team at Howard Books, my family, my teammates, all the women from Carswell who helped me in some way on my journey, and especially all my fans and supporters.

CONTENTS

CHAPTER 1

THE WAY BACK

As the cameras clicked and the videotapes rolled, I stepped up to a battalion of microphones stationed in front of the Westchester County Federal Courthouse in White Plains, New York. It was Friday, October 5, 2007, an unseasonably warm day. The treetops swayed with occasional gusts of wind. There was a long ribbon of people across the street, shouting "We love you, Marion." I didn't know any of them, but they were like angels sent from God to wrap their wings around me on one of the lowest days of my life.

My mother, other relatives, and close supporters stood behind me and around me like sturdy pillars. A swarm of reporters and photographers was arrayed on the steps of the brick-faced courthouse, all jockeying for spots near the microphones.

Moments earlier, I had been inside the building, standing before U.S. District Judge Kenneth Karas. Karas is a bespectacled man with a shock of brown hair and a stern, hard-nosed manner. His courtroom looked like something straight out of a legal drama, with wood-paneled walls, pews, and a sign above the judge's head that said "In God We Trust." It was filled to capacity with journalists from around the world. The proceeding was televised on closed-circuit television to a nearby overflow room.

I was stoic and scared at the same time. I pled guilty to two charges: lying in 2003 to federal investigators about my use of a performance-enhancing drug and lying to them about my knowledge of a separate check fraud case. In my guilty plea, I told the court that in September 2000, before the Sydney Olympic Games, a former coach first gave me a substance he told me was flaxseed oil. As it turned out, the "flaxseed oil" was a performance-enhancing drug (PED) now known as "the clear."

My eyes never strayed from Judge Karas's face. Whenever he uttered the ramifications of my guilty plea, using words like "prison," "felony," or "punishment," I simply said, "Yes, I understand." As he spoke, I thought of the shame I'd brought on my family, the sport of track and field, my former teammates, and my many supporters. I knew I'd spend a very long time trying to make up for the damage I'd caused.

Judge Karas said he wanted to schedule my sentencing hearing for January fourth. I leaned over to my attorneys and whispered that January fourth was my mother's birthday. They politely requested a different date. The judge complied and set my sentencing date for January 11, 2008.

The hearing lasted just thirty minutes. Judge Karas banged his gavel, and the courtroom cleared.

I was not only in emotional pain, but physical pain too. I was still breast-feeding my second son, Amir, who was home in Austin being cared for by my husband Obadele Thompson. I had packed my breast pump in my suitcase so I could pump milk and not become engorged, but a piece of the pump broke off during the trip. The pump wouldn't work, so I couldn't pump any milk. My breasts got so engorged that I thought they might explode. They started leaking. By the end of the hearing, my pink blouse, hidden thankfully under my dark pinstriped suit, was soaked with breast milk. My breasts hurt so much that it was painful to hug people.

Outside the courtroom, a crush of people awaited my statement, which I had written in the days leading up to my courtroom appearance. I took a deep breath. I did my best to make eye contact with all who were there.

"Good afternoon, everyone. I am Marion Jones-Thompson, and I am here today because I have something very important to tell you, my fans, my friends, and my family.

"Over the many years of my life as an athlete in the sport of track and field, you have been fiercely loyal and supportive towards me. Even more loyal and supportive than words can declare has been my family, and especially my dear mother, who stands by my side today."

I felt like crying, and then I did cry. I choked back the sobs, but

I could not hold back the tears. I was wracked with humiliation and then by free-floating remorse. I paused to regain my composure.

"And so it is with a great amount of shame that I stand before you and tell you that I have betrayed your trust," I continued, bowing my head briefly. "I want all you to know that today I pled guilty to two counts of making false statements to federal agents.

"Making these false statements to federal agents was an incredibly stupid thing for me to do, and I am fully responsible for my actions. I have no one to blame but myself for what I have done.

"To you, my fans—including my young supporters—the United States Track and Field Association, my closest friends, my attorneys, and the most classy family a person could ever hope for—namely my mother, my husband, my children, my brother and his family, my uncle, and the rest of my extended family: I want you to know that I have been dishonest. And you have the right to be angry with me."

By then I was sobbing so hard I could barely catch my breath. I bit my lip and went on.

"I have let them down. I have let my country down. And I have let myself down.

"I recognize that by saying that I'm deeply sorry, it might not be enough and sufficient to address the pain and the hurt that I have caused you. Therefore, I want to ask for your forgiveness for my actions, and I hope you can find it in your heart to forgive me.

"I have asked Almighty God for forgiveness.

"Having said this, and because of my actions, I am retiring from the sport of track and field, a sport which I deeply love."

My voice was cracking and tears streamed down my face.

"I promise that these events will be used to help make the lives of others improve, to show that making the wrong choices and bad decisions can be disastrous.

"I want to thank you all for your time."

I could see the hands clapping, but I barely heard the applause.

The calm strength I had tried to display in the courtroom was gone, washed away by a flood of tears. I embraced my mother and cried. We then threaded through the throng, climbed into an awaiting car with both of my attorneys, Hill Allen and Henry DePippo, and drove away without taking any questions.

But for me, questions remained. What would be my punishment? Would I go to jail? I prayed not. My young children and husband needed me.

My ordeal was what the media would call a "stunning fall from grace." For more than a decade, I had been hailed as the "the fastest woman on the planet." At the 2000 Olympic Games, I became the first woman ever to win five medals at one Olympics. That same year, the Associated Press and ESPN named me "Athlete of the Year." I was on the cover of *Vogue*, *Time*, *Newsweek*, and *Sports Illustrated*. I seemed to have it all—fame, fortune, talent, and international acclaim. Now it was gone—all of it, because I had exercised bad judgment, made bad decisions, and lied about it all when it was absolutely essential to tell the truth.

We drove away from the courthouse in silence. I rested my head against the seat back and stared vacantly out the window. There is an old African proverb that goes something like this: "A concealed disease can't be healed." Confession is always good for the soul. Deep down, I knew that my confession was the beginning of the healing process for me.

For most of us, the words "I'm sorry" are the two hardest words to say. I know they are for me. I used to assume that if I apologized, I'd show weakness. But it is just the opposite. I believe that most people appreciate honesty and the courage it takes to admit your own mistakes and failings. When I travel around the country now, people approach and tell me that they don't think they could have done what I did—admit that I had made mistakes and lied about it—because it's hard for them to own up to their wrongs privately, let alone do so publicly in front of the whole world. If we truly want or need forgiveness, we'll need to apologize. Apology begins the process of healing, correction, and restoration.

Events leading up to my downfall began four years earlier, in November 2003 . . .

———————◼———————

It began when I was subpoenaed by a federal grand jury in San Francisco to testify as a witness in a federal investigation—the now infamous Bay Area Laboratory Cooperative (BALCO) case—which was looking into, among other things, illegal steroid distribution.

In early September 2003, the feds raided the BALCO facilities and confiscated containers of performance-enhancing drugs (PEDs)—steroids, human growth hormone, synthetic testosterone—and files with the names of several professional athletes.

In June 2003, a coach anonymously sent a syringe containing traces of an unknown substance to the United States Anti-Doping Agency (USADA) for analysis. In August 2003, the USADA commissioned a renowned expert in performance-enhancing drugs to analyze the substance. He determined that the substance in the syringe was, in fact, a performance-enhancing drug known as THG. Because THG was undetectable in drug tests commonly administered to athletes, it was labeled "the clear."

Essentially, if athletes ingested THG, their urine would be "clear," and the drug would not show up in the test results. Apparently, "the clear" was one of the substances confiscated during the federal government's raid of the BALCO labs.

As a result of the raid, the federal grand jury in San Francisco subpoenaed some forty athletes, including me, baseball superstars Barry Bonds and Jason Giambi, several NFL players, and others to testify about BALCO and seek evidence to determine if the company was a front for an illegal steroid-distribution ring catering to elite athletes. My former boyfriend, then 100-meter world-record holder Tim Montgomery, was also scheduled to appear before the grand jury.

After I was served with my subpoena, my attorneys, Rich Nichols and Joe Burton, spent three eight-hour sessions prepping me for what the AUSA, the federal investigator, and up to twenty-four grand jurors, composed of citizens selected from voter registration, driver's license, and tax lists, might ask me. My attorneys, Joe and Rich, are long-time, trusted friends who specialize in white-collar defense and legal management. They both impressed upon me that a federal grand jury appearance is "serious stuff." You never know what questions will be fired at you. The grand jury system by its nature is highly secretive, and everyone fears it. Above all, you MUST tell the truth!

Ten days prior to my scheduled grand jury appearance, Rich and Joe made a strategic decision. They reached out to the government and offered to present me to the AUSA and the federal investigator for a pre-grand jury appearance interview. The purpose: to have an opportunity to see what information the government possessed prior to my grand jury appearance and to get a feel for the questions the government might ask me in the grand jury. The risk with such an interview: if you lie to the AUSA and the federal agent during the interview, you could be prosecuted for lying to them and you can be sent to jail.

So, to encourage truth telling during these interviews, the government gives witnesses like me one-day immunity in the form of an agreement called a "queen for a day" letter. Essentially, this letter is a written agreement between federal prosecutors and individuals that permits these individuals to be questioned by the federal agents *not* under oath and without the risk of being prosecuted for anything the witness tells the government during the interview. Thus, under this procedure, no matter what you tell them, they can't use what you tell them during the interview to prosecute you, ever.

But here's the catch: You can't lie during a queen-for-a-day session, because making false statements to federal agents, even if not under oath, is a felony offense. You must tell the truth, or risk prosecution for lying. My attorneys explained this to me, over and over.

The feds rarely grant queen-for-a-day sessions, but they did in my case. These sessions are risky business, but we were relieved when the government granted our request to meet with them at the Fairmont Hotel in San Jose.

On that early November morning, my attorneys and I walked into the windowed conference room, with its magnificent panorama of San Jose's sprawl. The room was elegantly neutral with beige walls, finely upholstered chairs, and a carved mahogany table neatly set with bottled water. I didn't know what to expect. What did they want from me? What do they think I know? I was nervous, very nervous.

We had been in the conference room for several minutes when I heard the click of the door handle. Striding into the conference room, the assistant U.S. attorney (the AUSA) and the federal agent Jeff Novitsky looked like infantry soldiers prepared to do battle. Novitsky was a six-foot, six-inch, lanky former college basketball player from California with a glistening white bald head. He had initiated the government's probe into an illegal steroid distribution case and had a reputation for badgering witnesses. They took their seats directly across from Rich, Joe, and me.

The interview started out on a perfunctory note, inquisition style, but not long into the meeting, I began to feel the ooze of provocation and hostility seeping from them.

Novitsky had a brownish leather duffle bag on the floor next to his chair. For two and a half hours, he'd pull documents from the bag and shove them across the table at me. With each document, he'd say, "Do you recognize this?" His speech became increasingly clipped and rapid.

I'd respond "no" in a practiced voice, one trained to stay calm and confident in the face of accusation and allegation. I didn't feel like I had anything to hide. As the meeting progressed, I could tell they didn't believe me. They'd ask me the same question over and over, but in different ways. The less my information satisfied them, the more frustrated they got.

Then Novitsky reached into the duffle bag and retrieved two plastic baggies. In one of the baggies was a vial of liquid that looked like light olive oil, in the other, an unlabeled tube of cream. He dangled the baggie with the vial in front of me. "Do you recognize this?

When I saw the substance, of course it could have been anything—

the oil I cook with, the oil I used to get from pricking vitamin E capsules to apply on my pimples as a teenager, anything. But I wondered if it was THG, "the clear," that everyone had been talking about in the news.

From across the table, Novitsky stared at me, contemptuous and unblinking. I had one of those "Oh my God" moments and figured out that yes, it was the clear—a liquid that I believed to be flaxseed oil when I had taken it in September 2000, before and following the 2000 Sydney Olympic Games.

I got a deep, cold feeling inside. Admitting I had used it would be disastrous. My mind at that instant was a snapshot of everything I stood to lose if I revealed the truth—my child's future, my reputation, my earning power, my athletic career. I decided to lie—and lie willingly.

"No sir, I don't recognize it."

He shook the baggie in front of my face. "You mean to tell me you don't know what this is?"

I lied again. "No, I do not."

Novitsky glowered at me. "Have you ever taken performance-enhancing drugs?"

"No, I have not." Another lie.

"Have you ever taken a performance-enhancing drug known as 'the clear'?"

I swallowed hard and lied again. "No."

Novitsky abruptly stood up and angrily shook the baggie again. "I know you know something." His tenacity struck me as comparable to that of a pit bull that had been taunted.

At that point, Joe Burton quickly leaned his fireplug of a body forward. With furrowed eyebrows that peered over his wire-rimmed glasses, he called time out. Rich, a wiry bundle of intelligence and energy, stood up first, signaling his solidarity with Joe. The four men hustled outside the conference room and closed the door.

I shifted in my chair, allowed my shoulders to sink an inch or two, and stared into nothingness. I sold myself on my lies, for the same reasons that a lot of people do: I had done something wrong, I did not want to be found out, and I was frightened of the consequences and repercussions if the truth was revealed. I could not steel-cage my fear. I was frightened at a level more primal than I would have imagined. I feared that my life and the life of my young son, Monty, would be forever changed if the truth were known. I feared losing my athletic career—all I had ever known— and I was too insecure to believe that I could do anything else with my life outside of running track. Lying was a form of self-protection. All the hard work and the sacrifices I had made since I was a kid would be gone in the blink of a moment if I told the truth. I couldn't let that happen. My answers were not going to change.

Thirty seconds later, the men filed back into the conference room. The questioning resumed, and tension still hung in the air.

In forced, overdetermined civility, Novitsky asked me again, "Look a little closer. Do you know what this is?"

"No sir, I do not know what it is."

And then, as abruptly as we began, we were done.

When the session was over, I found myself in the precarious position of having lied to the U.S. attorney and to the federal agent about recognizing the substance they showed me. I did recognize it. And I had made that lie even worse by continuing to lie even when I put the pieces together in a flash while sitting in that conference room. What I had been given as a nutritional supplement was, indeed, "the clear," or THG.

When people ask me, "How could you unknowingly take a performance-enhancing drug?" The answer boils down to the trust factor between athletes and coaches. If a coach comes to an athlete and says, "Take this nutritional supplement; it might help your performance," you do it. You trust your coach implicitly.

You have to understand that as an elite, world-class athlete, competing at the highest levels, you rely on your coach to be your ultimate caretaker. Your coach prescribes your training programs, nutritional supplements, competition schedules, advice with regard to general nutrition, physical therapy, and rest and recovery.

As an athlete who has had coaches all my life, I learned early on that you just don't question your coach, ever. The best way to alienate coaches is to complain about their recommendations. Coaches are like a mother, father, big brother, best friend—all in one. They're dedicated to you, and so you run through the proverbial wall for them every day—in training and practice and in every competition during the season.

In the months that followed, I thought my lie would settle quietly in my mind and, like a bad dream, fade away, but I was wrong. Lies don't go away, and I could not run from mine. Left uncorrected, lies have a way of getting bigger and taking on a life of their own. More lies are told, or the truth remains hidden to protect the lies already told.

Some people might say: "It's no big deal; everybody lies." Well then, how come when we are lied to, we generally feel betrayed and outraged? Because the longer a lie goes unchecked, the more a person's character is called into question when the truth is revealed.

A lie usually ends up hurting the person who told it more than anyone else. There are always consequences to lying, and they certainly can be unpleasant and even ugly. If you lie on a job application, your employer may be mad, but it is your career and your reputation that is hurt. If you lie to a friend or your family, your relationship with them is damaged, and the trust they had in you disappears and is extremely difficult to get back again. If you lie about large issues like I did—something like a crime or legal offense—you may be painfully punished, and it is hard to heal.

I learned the hard way that it's always better to tell the truth. That may seem like advice my little Monty hears in kindergarten, but the fact is that a huge percentage of us are too comfortable with lying in many ways. When we are deceitful like I was, deceit has a habit of coming back to haunt us, and in these situations, we are worse off than if we had just come clean in the first place—as uncomfortable as that might have seemed at the time. Lying rarely ever achieves what we hope it will. Somewhere, sometime, someone will find out, and then we have to deal with the hurt, anger, and pain that usually follow.

Another thing I've learned about lies is what they want: they want out. The truth is like a beach ball being held under water. It will go down, but it won't stay under. It constantly tries to rise to the surface. Keeping truth submerged robs a person of integrity, credibility, confidence, peace, and self-esteem.

I had even ensnared people who trusted me into my web of lies—and unknowingly, they lied for me. "She has never taken performance-enhancing drugs, not now, not ever," Rich Nichols once declared in a statement to the media.

Looking back, I didn't love myself enough to tell the truth. I thought I was hiding a lie, but really my lie was hiding me. I was too focused on what I did rather than who God created me to be. What we do is important, but what we do ultimately emanates from who we are. I've since learned to spend more time on building my character than on building my athletic skills. We can be much more successful in the long run if our skills are high and our character is even higher.

To this day, I still say to myself, "If only I had told the truth . . ." I know now that it's better to be honest and accept responsibility the way you'd take care of a training injury: fast, thoroughly, with no messing around. This means fully admitting a mistake, apologizing to anyone you may have harmed by your actions, and making any amends you possibly can.

There are the times in our lives when we know we are making the wrong choice. In my case, I wish I had taken a break that day in the Fairmont Hotel conference room, cleared my mind, analyzed my options with my attorneys, and told the truth—in other words, I wish I had done the right thing and gotten on the right track.

The consequences of my actions would never leave me. For a few years, though, it felt as if my life were returning to a semblance of normal. But it wasn't, not really.

CHAPTER 2

A LIFE OF TRIUMPH AND TRAGEDY

For those of you who know me, I suppose you can fast-forward through the next few paragraphs, but for those who don't, I am Marion Jones, and I have lived a life of triumph and tragedy.

I was born in 1975 in Los Angeles, the daughter of George Jones—who was a businessman—and Marion, a hardworking legal secretary who had moved to the United States from Belize in 1968 at age twenty-two. I have one brother, Albert Kelly. Albert is five years older than me. I look up to him. He is my great and lasting hero, and we have always been close. Albert has always believed in me.

I was around four years old when my father walked out and abandoned our family. He and my mom divorced, and the three of us were on our own. Thereafter, George spurned my attempts to be a part of his life. My brother did his best to fill the void as the only man in the house when we were young.

Back then, I was young and could not understand everything. There was a lot of pain and confusion in my heart, and I did not

17

know how to deal with it properly. So, over the next few years, I started acting out and getting in trouble at school. My mom tried her best with me, but I was definitely a handful. At that time, I couldn't appreciate how much sacrifice she made for my brother and me. We were not poor, but we were very aware of how hard our mom worked to give us the things we needed and some of things we wanted. My mom worked two jobs to have enough money to provide for us. And she would often drive over an hour and a half between her job, our school, and home. She loved me, but in many ways, that love was overshadowed by the lack of real love from my biological father.

As a spunky five-year-old, I started chasing Albert around the neighborhood. It took not only speed, but my outrageous competitive nature to keep up with him and his pals, who didn't want to have anything to do with me. They considered me a pest. But finally, they gave in and let me play in their games, races, and other sports.

Mom married a wonderful man named Ira Toler, and we settled in a growing suburb of Los Angeles called Palmdale, California. Albert and I finally learned about the stability of a two-parent home. Ira took us to school, to baseball practice, and to gymnastics. He was the type of father who would bring McDonald's to my school at lunch time and have dinner ready for us every night. A retired military chef, he was a great cook and we always had delicious leftovers. You couldn't find a better individual, a better human being, a better father than Ira Toler. When he smiled, he grabbed a piece of your heart.

A defining moment for me occurred in 1984, when the Summer

Olympics came to Los Angeles. I was eight years old. Ira drove me to the Los Angeles Memorial Coliseum to see the parade for the opening ceremonies. I saw the torch and felt this wonderful excitement mounting because the Olympics were going to start and the best athletes in the world were there.

I watched the rest of the Olympics at home with my parents on television. By the end, I was enthralled with track and field. When I saw the athletes actually cross the finish line, the excitement in their faces, and the glimmer in their eyes, I wanted to feel whatever was causing that expression. I wanted that experience.

My mom and Ira hung a chalkboard in my room for my homework. I erased all those homework assignments and instead wrote on the board that I would become an Olympic champion someday.

That's the can-do spirit with which my mother raised us. Anything you wanted in life, you wrote it down. You thought about it, you believed it, and then you went out and did whatever it took to accomplish it. She taught us that you can achieve what you believe.

After competing against my brother and his friends for so long, racing against girls my own age was nothing. I began entering competitions at the age of ten and won everything. That's when I began to believe I had something very special.

For a school assignment, I wrote my first biography on the ruled lines of my homework paper. It went something like this: "Hi, my name is Marion Jones. I'm five feet two inches. I am ten years old and in the sixth grade. I think I have a nice personality. I have pretty good grades and my weight is eighty-five pounds. My hobbies are running and gymnastics. I like running because I can beat almost everyone at my school. I like gymnastics because I can do all sort of tricks and I'm very flexible in some ways. My plans for the future are to be in the 1992 Olympics. I've been training a lot, and the boys at my school are good practice. I know if I don't get in the Olympics, I have to have a backup. So I plan to be an electrical engineer like my uncle."

One morning in 1985, when I was in school, the phone rang in the classroom, and my teacher told me, "Marion, your mother is up front. She's taking you home." Mom told me that when she'd returned from dropping me off at school, Ira had been lying on the ground. She'd called an ambulance. Ira had had a stroke.

I don't know how long he stayed alive—a day and a half or so. At that time, the hospital didn't allow minor children in to see critically ill patients. I was ten. I was so upset that Mom promised she'd persuade the nurse to sneak me in. But it never happened. I never saw Ira again, except at his funeral. Ira's death was one of the saddest experiences of my life.

Sports were a way to cope and gave me a chance to realize myself as a person. I eventually became one of California's top high school basketball players and sprinters. I had wonderful coaches along the way—Geoff Jarvis, Al Walker, Wise, Mel Sims, Art Green, Charles Brown, and Elliot Mason. They all have a special place in my heart. From them, I learned discipline, patience, focus, cooperation, and the ideals of good sportsmanship—the fundamentals required to become a champion. I grew up to be five feet ten, which was taller than almost everyone I knew.

At the U.S. Olympic Track and Field Trials for the 1992 Barcelona Olympic Games, I finished fourth in the 200 meters and sixth in the 100 meters, and I qualified as an alternate for the 400-meter relay team. I was sixteen. My mom and I didn't think I was quite ready for the Olympics, though. I wanted to earn my own gold medal through sweat and hard work, not get one just for running in a relay preliminary. I decided not to go. I took college prep math classes at a local university instead.

Basketball was my other sport, and I was the California Division I player of the year as a high school senior. Hundreds of colleges recruited me, most of them for track only. I chose the University of North Carolina at Chapel Hill because they would let me play basketball too. The track establishment was appalled, convinced I was jeopardizing my future Olympic prospects. The criticism only fueled my desire to prove them wrong. Nobody was going to tell me I couldn't play basketball and run track at the same time.

As a freshman point guard, I helped take the Lady Tar Heels to a 35–2 record and a national championship. In my three seasons there, North Carolina was 92–10.

My track career at UNC had its ups and downs. In my freshman year, I placed second at a major competition in the long jump, but placed only sixth in the 200 and failed to make the 100-meter final. Basically, I was running slower than my high school times. I chalked up my slump to playing an entire basketball season and getting in just a week of practice before I was thrown into track competitions. Obviously, there was no way I could win. It was a lack of track and field training. After all, my priority was basketball, and I was on a basketball scholarship. Track would have to wait until I recovered from basketball and was ready to go out there.

After college, I began competing in track meets and rededicated myself to track. I took it one step at a time. I knew that if I didn't create barriers and limits for myself, anything was possible. I joined a training group called Sprint Capitol USA in Raleigh, North Carolina. I had realistic goals and started to make my mark. I had an amazing year in 1998. I became the fastest woman in the world in the 100 and 200 meters and the first woman in fifty years to win the 100, the 200, and long jump in the same U.S. Championships. I won every race I entered that year. I earned nearly one million dollars that year in winnings and endorsements.

I set my sights on a feat never before accomplished by a woman: to win five gold medals at the 2000 Games in Sydney. I knew it would test my mind, my body, and my spirit, but I felt in my heart I could do it.

During my very first Olympic race, the 100-meter dash, the gun fired, and I exploded out of the blocks. I won in 10.75 seconds, with the second-greatest margin of victory for a 100-meter race in Olympic history. In the coming days, I ended up winning gold in the 100 meters, 200 meters and 4 × 400 meters relay. But the remainder of my quest didn't pan out. I took the bronze in the long jump and 4×100 relay. Still, I was the first woman to win five track and field medals in a single Olympics.

It seemed that overnight I was famous. I had multimillion-dollar development deals, corporate sponsors galore, and plenty of recognition from people everywhere.

But from all that fame and glory, my life started unraveling. I was trying to get past two failed relationships. I had an acrimonious split with my track coach. In 2003, allegations of my use of performance-enhancing drugs before the Sydney Olympics began to swirl, and before long, I became the focus and poster child of the biggest doping scandal in history.

Now, looking back, maybe I needed what happened to me. Maybe I needed to have my face plastered on the front of the newspapers. Maybe I needed to be an item on the nightly news. Maybe I needed the pain, the hurt, the humiliation. The purpose of all of it was to make me honest—really honest . . . and most importantly, honest and true to myself and to God. I needed it to learn that, in life, we must be truthful and do what's right.

We don't always think of the consequences of bad choices, and how they can hold us captive. And if they're colossally bad choices, like the ones I've made, they can tear your mind apart and wreck your spirit.

After I lied to federal prosecutors, I thought everything was all right. I thought I could handle it. I thought I could deal with it. I thought I could live with it. I thought it wouldn't wear me out. But it wore me out and it wore me down. I was living under a weight that I couldn't get off my back until I cleaned up the mess of my life.

I should be clear about why I'm writing this book. If you picked it up looking for salacious details about doping and drug scandals, I guess you should put it back on the shelf. This is my story, and my story is about my mistakes, how I came to grips with them, the consequences of my actions, and how I made meaning from all of it. My story is different from the one you read in magazines, newspaper, tabloids, or watch on a sports cable channel. My story is about confronting your mistakes, taking responsibility, picking yourself up, moving forward, and doing what you were uniquely created by God to do.

No one is exempt from making mistakes. We all fall down. We all have regret over some action. We let ourselves get knocked down by bad decisions, bad choices, or just by life itself. It's those knocks that give us the knowledge and the strength to pick ourselves up with God's help.

None of us has to walk around in shame because of some mistake or indiscretion we've committed in our lives. There is a lesson in every mistake. I am as thankful for the valleys as I am for the mountaintops. I am thankful for the storms as well as the sunshine. It is in the valley and through the storm that we find our way back.

It's what you do after the mistake that really matters, after all. That's what defines your legacy. We can take our experiences and grow from them, move beyond the shame of them, and use what they have taught us. When you start understanding this, you can live your life with greater joy and purpose.

I have often thought of my eventual decision to tell the truth and have marveled at how the most painful period of my life began a journey to freedom. You know the old saying, "The truth will set you free"? It's true, and you will feel better when you are no longer living a lie. My faith teaches me that God loves us unconditionally, but it also teaches me that He is a jealous God who loves us too much to leave us mired in our sin and confusion. He uses our own bad choices and disappointments to refine us like gold held over fire. Telling the truth about our brokenness is at the heart of an authentic faith. Telling the truth gives us a new heart and a right spirit.

It's not easy for me to talk about the mistakes I've made. But as I thought about what I'd like to do with my life, I felt that people might be able to learn from my mistakes. I decided I wanted to make a difference in the lives of others—to help people get on the right track so that they can avoid adversity caused by bad choices. I want to help people turn their lives around, no matter how far they have fallen. What happened to me could happen to anyone. If even one person could be helped by my example, then all my struggles have been worth it. I want to inspire others by the fact that if even an Olympic medalist who earned millions and was on the cover of *Vogue* could fall to such depths and then rise up and see a new day then they could have a new start too. For the first time, I had a new dream that was consuming me. It was something I felt strongly about. I felt that God wanted me to do it and had equipped me to do it.

Maybe there are those of who are wondering, "How can there possibly be a purpose for my life?" Maybe you've had disappointments at times or no real direction in your life. I'm well aware that there are those who have had traumatizing experiences. Sometimes God will let us fall flat on our face because it won't be until we fall flat that we have reason to get up, stronger, wiser, and better than before. That is what happened to me.

My prayer is that my story will help you gather up the strength, the confidence, and the courage to see your way through any experience, no matter how rocky, and see that every situation can inspire a positive step forward.

CHAPTER 3

WE BECOME THE DECISIONS WE MAKE

In September 2000, before the Olympics in Sydney, my coach began providing me with a substance he told me was flaxseed oil, a nutritional substance.

He told me to put it under my tongue for a few seconds, then swallow. I took it along with multivitamins, vitamin C, vitamin E, amino acids, and whey protein—the stuff most athletes take.

I was told not to tell anyone anything about what I was given or about my workouts or training. Being told to keep quiet should have tipped me off. But I still went along with it. I didn't question anything. A fatal flaw of mine is that I've always been a little naive, much too trusting. When I hired coaches, I trusted that they had my best interests in mind. I believed with all my heart that coaches would never do anything to hurt their athletes, especially giving them dangerous and performance-enhancing drugs. After all, if something bad happened to the athlete, it would harm the coach and everyone in the training group. A coach would never risk that, or so I reasoned.

27

I was compliant—a coach's dream. You didn't have to tell me something twice. "Just tell me, I'll do it"—that was my way of being coached. So dutifully, I took the flaxseed oil.

I should have been more careful. Athletes have to know exactly what we put in our bodies. We have to know what the banned substances are, because we're liable. It doesn't matter whether you knew or didn't know—you are responsible for everything you put in your body.

The list of banned substances for track athletes reads like the inventory of a pharmacy. It's voluminous and comprehensive, and track and field athletes are charged with the absolute responsibility to know what drugs are on the banned substance list. There are so many that the U.S. Track and Field Association prepares a wallet-sized card that we can carry with us, or we can refer to the organization's website for the list.

Doping can take on many forms in sports. Taking performance-enhancing drugs (PEDs) is probably the most well-known method of doping, and the best known kind of PED is a class of drug called steroids. THG (the "clear") is a steroid. Steroids are drugs that have testosterone as their base. Medicinally, when prescribed by doctors, steroids are administered to patients to promote healing and sometimes muscle and tissue regeneration. Steroids can increase aggression, muscle strength, size, and power. Some steroids can provide athletes the ability to train harder and recover more quickly from strenuous workouts. But taking steroids can cause devastating side effects, such as liver or kidney tumors, cancer, and high blood pressure. Since 1990, it has been illegal to use steroids in the United States without a doctor's prescription. Steroids were banned from the Olympics and college sports more than thirty years ago.

I'm no expert on doping, but one thing that all world-class track and field athletes necessarily become experts on is the drug-testing process to which we are all subjected.

Track athletes are subject to both in-competition drug testing and out-of-competition drug testing. Track and field has the most stringent drug-testing policy of any sport, and it is a tough, laborious, and stressful protocol. At every single track meet, after we cross the finish line, a drug-testing chaperone, one per competitor, greets us to escort us to a drug-testing area. We have forty-five minutes to report there. If we fail to show up, we can be charged with a doping violation. When we check in to the drug-testing facility, which is usually located less than a half-mile from the track, we have to fill out a detailed form, listing any and all medicinal-type substances we consumed that day—everything from Gatorade to aspirin, to whatever. We are then led to sit in an observation room monitored by drug testing officials who watch us and make sure we don't surreptitiously take any substances prior to providing our urine sample. We're offered water, juice, or sometimes beer to boost our ability to urinate. When we feel like urinating, our delegated drug testing official goes into the bathroom with us and literally watches us urinate into the bottles to make sure that it is actually our genuine urine. Providing a urine sample can take a few minutes or several hours. You can't leave until you have gone in the bottles.

We urinate into two separate containers and personally affix the seal cap on each container of urine. The containers are about six inches tall and made from a hard plastic material. Both containers are sealed tightly. One container is referred to as the "A" sample; the other, the "B" sample. Each sample is assigned a corresponding serial number. The serial number corresponds to your name. We fill out more forms confirming that the urine samples in the A and B containers are in fact our own. Finally, we are allowed to inspect each container to make sure the seal is satisfactorily tight. Satisfied that all is okay with the samples, we sign our names on the form. Identified by serial numbers only—not our names, the samples are sent off to the testing lab.

The A sample is usually the only batch that is analyzed for drugs. If the A sample tests negatively, meaning no drugs are detected in an athlete's system, we don't hear anything. If the A sample comes back positive for the presence of a banned substance, then an athlete is notified by letter. By track and field rules, the only entities entrusted with this information are the athlete, his or her representative, the governing organization of the sport, and the United States and International Olympic Committees. Otherwise, the test results of the A sample must remain confidential. At that point, we have the option to have our B sample tested. If the B sample turns up positive, the athlete is charged with a doping violation. We can be disqualified from competition for two years if we're caught once, and then banned for life if caught a second time.

Out-of-competition drug testing can occur any time and any place—at work, home, the track, the gym, in class, or in any public place—in the United States and abroad. These tests can be taken at random and without notice. We have to notify the drug testing officials of our whereabouts at all times. If you're not where you said you would be when the drug testers show up to administer an unannounced drug test, you can be sanctioned.

I remember once, while I was on my way to the airport, rushing to get on a plane, I was notified that I had to give a urine sample for a drug test. I stood inside a crowded bathroom stall at the airport and urinated into a container. I say "crowded," because a representative from the anti-doping agency squeezed inside the stall with me. Again, a rigorous, but necessary system.

These days, when I talk to kids at schools, they ask me about PEDs. I explain that all of the banned substances give athletes an unnatural advantage. In sports, there's always an attempt to get an edge. But I tell kids that doing more weight training and extra laps of the track, taking care of their bodies, and getting enough sleep gives you the edge—not the use of performance-enhancing drugs.

Track athletes do a lot to give them a natural advantage in hopes of winning—from learning new start techniques to wearing high-tech shoes designed to provide support and stability, minimize shock, and reduce fatigue.

And yes, we visualize success. One of my favorite stories about visualization concerns the legendary track and field star Jim Thorpe. In 1912, while other American athletes worked out on a cork track on the deck of the ocean liner bound for the Olympics in Stockholm, Jim Thorpe sat in a chair and dozed.

When a reporter asked what he was doing, Thorpe replied: "I'm practicing the broad jump. I just jumped twenty-three feet, eight inches." (That was a lot back then; today, track athletes can jump nearly thirty feet.)

After arriving in Stockholm, Thorpe continued his peculiar regimen—lying in a hammock and visualizing. It paid off. Thorpe dominated the games. He possessed the ability to achieve amazing feats with his body by harnessing the power of his mind.

In order to win five Olympic medals in the Sydney Olympic Games, I followed Jim Thorpe's lead. I worked hard and visualized my success. But I lost it all because I did not ask questions when I should have been inquisitive, and I misplaced my trust in someone I believed had my best interests at heart.

But to sum up, the "winning edge" is really a combination of hard work, execution, discipline, inborn talent, and the belief that you will succeed. This is how I lived my athletic life. From the time I was ten years old, I dominated track and field events. I was always getting better because I was training and practicing, practicing and training—all the time. I was always aware that somebody was out there trying to beat me. Somebody was out there training while I was at home, so I made sure to get out there and train. That way, I could leave the track every day knowing that I trained better than anyone else in the world on that particular day. Very few people can outtrain me!

The reality is that I was born fast. Nothing was going to make me faster, except talent and training. In fact, I ran my fastest times in the 100 meters and 200 meters in 1998, long before the BALCO scandal. Those performances are still in the official record books. If you look at me and look at my life, I'm living proof that you are limited only by your inborn gifts and talents. Within those bounds, whatever you want to do, you can do it. We determine our own destiny, that's the bottom line.

In 2002, my body did change, though. I felt sluggish. I wasn't able to recover. I didn't understand why, but I chalked it up to a change in my training regimen. At first I wasn't worried, but when the fatigue got worse, I went straight to my doctor.

The doctor did tests for viruses, blood-sugar levels, for this and that, but the only test that came up positive was one I hadn't asked for. "You're pregnant," my doctor said.

I was incredulous and excited at the same time. I always wanted to be a mom. And now I was pregnant. The father was my then-boyfriend, Tim Montgomery.

I wasn't due to give birth until later in July, but delivered a five-pound, fourteen-ounce boy on June 28, 2003, at Duke University Hospital in Raleigh, North Carolina. I named him Monty.

The instant after the cord was cut, I was holding him and gazing into his beautiful, saucer-like brown eyes. I'll never forget the look he gave me—not the sleepy look I thought I'd see, but a wide smile that expressed, "So you're my mommy!"

Monty's birth gave new meaning to my life. Prior to having him, I was preoccupied with some of the things I had been through, whether they were good or bad. But I think that having him helped my sense of almost everything. New parenthood will bring you the greatest joy you'll ever feel, and being a mother is the single best job I will ever have.

After Monty's birth, I adjusted to life at home with a newborn. I had decided to give myself a month off and allow my body to recover before I started training again for the 2004 Olympic Games.

My plan was to get on with the business of living my life. But it was not to be. My decision to not ask questions about the flaxseed oil would come back to haunt me.

Yes, I took a performance-enhancing drug and I can't go back and undo any of it. What happened, happened. I'm not holding anyone responsible for the fact that I'm the one who put it in my body. I'm not bitter, I'm not pointing fingers, and I don't hold any grudges. Nobody forced me. At the end of the day, I was the one who made the decision to trust, not ask questions, and then ultimately lie when confronted with the truth.

CHAPTER 4

BLINDSIDED

By 2004, I was floating along the gentle sea of denial about my lie, buoyed by the blind hope that I could still achieve more in the sport. It was not to be.

I made the 2004 United States Olympic Track and Field Team that competed in Athens, but I had a poor showing. I finished a disappointing fifth in the long jump, even though I was pretty good in that event. I was once the top-ranked women's long jumper.

Then, I was involved in a botched baton pass in the U.S. women's 4 × 100-meters relay. I strained to hand over the baton several times. "Wait!" I screamed. "Hold up!" It was too late. My teammate Lauryn Williams had started her run too soon and was already out of the exchange zone.

I left the arena through the stadium tunnel, my eyes welling up in tears. I never figured things would turn out so badly. Nobody plans to fail. Nobody starts a race planning to finish poorly. I was devastated.

Athletically, this period of my life was a slump. I bounced around from coach to coach, but couldn't find anyone who could push me hard enough to achieve results.

And personally, there was a storm gathering, but I didn't see it.

As it turned out, a check I received from Tim Montgomery was part of a massive check-fraud scheme to cash up to $5 million in stolen, altered, or counterfeit checks through a network of New York counterfeiters. Without asking questions, I endorsed the check.

I was eventually questioned in August and September of 2006 by federal investigators because I had endorsed that check. Even though the U.S. attorney assured me that they knew I was not a part of the check fraud scheme, they needed to know what, if anything, I knew about the check I had received and its origins. Once again, I panicked. I did not want my name associated with that mess. I wanted to stay as far away from it as possible. When questioned, I lied about my knowledge of the check and Tim's involvement in the scheme.

For a good part of my athletic career, I lived in a bubble, far removed from friends and family and following bad advice. I could see the outside world but I wasn't part of it, because I allowed the men in my life to do everything for me. It was so bad that practically everything I did was based on them.

These experiences have weighed heavily on my mind. They left me more guarded and fearful but also a lot stronger than I ever believed I could be. I am now able to talk about my flaws—something I couldn't do for a long time because I felt so ashamed and embarrassed.

The upshot of all this is that, admittedly, I surrounded myself with the wrong people, especially men, and I blame myself for not being more discerning about those with whom I've associated over the years.

One reason I believe I've made poor decisions about men is because of unresolved issues that date back to when I was a kid. I lived all those years of my childhood, of growing up, without a father. My mom raised me and my older brother Albert as a single parent. When she married Ira Toler, I thought we had the perfect family. He was like the father I never had, and he showered me with love and taught me the right way.

But after Ira passed away, my mom was forced to be both mother and father for us. I've been searching for a father figure ever since, and I wonder if I won all those trophies and medals to impress the men in my life.

Eventually, I had to fight to get back the identity of who I was. As women, we often find ourselves in relationships that are so self-absorbing that we no longer have time for family, friends, or ourselves. We unrealistically tend to believe that this or that person is going to fulfill every need we have. Many of us need to use better judgment and make more sound decisions—about men and relationships, about our choices in life, about friends, and about how we deal with business associates.

The biggest blow after some of my failed relationships was my inability to trust my own judgment with men the next time around. If

I had made the wrong calls before, how would I even begin to make that decision again?

I was vulnerable, hungry for love, and insecure. At the same time, I was rebellious, ambitious, and wanted to go my own way—a real contradiction that got me into trouble. I was willing to trust anyone who was willing to prop me up and make me feel good about myself. In the end, I made countless bad decisions about who to trust in every facet of my life, and it cost me dearly.

We've all felt the pull of negative peer pressure, and adults aren't immune to it. But hanging with losers can influence our decisions and behavior. It takes the place of rational judgment.

What I've learned is to choose people whose company is enjoyable, supportive, and affirming. Drop those who belittle, betray, or hurt you. Cultivating supportive friendships will not only enrich your life, but deliver a healing power when you need it most. If you want to avoid trouble and make the best choices for your life, watch who you regularly associate with. Now I find myself being much more truthful about what it is I really want. And I now realize that the advice of people with experience must not be pushed aside.

Romantic relationships can be the toughest. Sometimes you don't want to take the chance on loving again because it's too painful. You're afraid you'll get hurt. I understand—been there, done that. But I can tell you this: taking a chance might be God's way of setting you up for something great. If you haven't struggled through the heartache, how can you appreciate the happiness?

Thankfully, happiness entered my life in the form of Obadele Thompson, or Oba, for short. At the end of 2005, after years of knowing each other on the professional track circuit, we began to develop a closer relationship. Oba was a track and field star in his own right and a hero in his home country of Barbados; he won the 100 meter bronze medal in Sydney. We trained together while I was living in North Carolina. Oba intrigued me. He was everything I thought he was. He was kind, unselfish, positive, smart, funny, mature, loving, comfortable, supportive, communicative, honest, and spiritual. I couldn't believe a man like this existed! My faith was not very strong at the time, and so I was drawn to his wonderful heart.

Looking back now, I see a pattern in how I used to behave with men. I tended to pursue difficult relationships that, in the end, would always be disastrous. But my relationship with Oba was different. He wasn't a bad boy like the others with a lot of drama; our relationship was healthy and stable. In fact, he gave me an unconditional, unselfish love I had never felt before. I wanted to grow old with this man. I suddenly knew that if I let go of fear, let go of the "should I?" and simply let myself love and be loved in return, happiness just might follow. The more time I spent with Oba, the more I wanted to be with him, and I found myself falling in love.

I was the first to say, "I love you." Our romance blossomed from there.

In 2006, Oba invited me to meet his parents, Hilda and Alvin, who lived in Barbados. That's when I got the feeling we were heading toward true coupledom. Barbados is so beautiful, with its white sandy beaches on the Caribbean side of the rugged eastern terrain carved by the Atlantic Ocean. Oba's childhood home is in Saint Michael, site of the country's capital, Bridgetown.

Oba's parents are a charming couple who love the Lord. Hilda is talkative and loving; Alvin is quiet and unassuming. Understandably, Hilda was curious about me. She'd watch me at night when I contacted Monty through a webcam to see how he was doing. We'd blow kisses at each other, sing songs, and chat animatedly. She watched all of this closely, and I think she was touched by what she saw. I ended up having a wonderful time, and I felt really close to Oba and his family.

Then I found out I was pregnant.

I was nervous about telling Oba because he didn't have any children. But instead of freaking out, we prayed about it and together decided that this was a blessing in our lives.

When we shared the news with his parents they were overjoyed. Oba was their "baby" and now their baby was going to have a baby.

Oba and I were married on February 24, 2007, in a tiny white chapel in rural Wilson Mills, North Carolina, with about one hundred guests, mostly family and close friends. Oba's uncle, Reverend Vibert Tyrrel, pastor of the church, officiated.

As I walked down the aisle on my wedding day, I looked ahead. I saw Oba standing there at the end of the aisle. When our eyes met, they got misty; both of us were overwhelmed with happiness. Monty at age three was one of the ring bearers, and a restless one at that. He got so fidgety—he didn't care that there was a wedding going on—that I had to pick him and hold him while Oba and I recited our vows.

Oba and his mom were in the delivery room with me when Amir was born on June 9, 2007. I have photographs of the first time Oba looked at Amir, as he lay newly born in his father's arms. The second he looked into Amir's wondering eyes, Oba cherished him. And I saw it again: the miracle of life.

Before Amir was even born, Oba and I watched videos together about pregnancy, childbirth, and nurturing a newborn. Immediately after the birth, Oba and his mom took care of everything until I was able to get back on my feet. They did all the laundry, cooking, and cleaning. Oba had very little experience with babies, so he was timid at first. But he learned fast, becoming an expert at feeding, burping, and that dreaded diapering. He also became a master at deciphering Amir's cries, and always jumped out of bed in the middle of the night to soothe him. Anyone will tell you that he is a great dad, but the truth lies in Amir's sparkling eyes and his huge grin whenever Oba comes into the room.

Oba picked the name, Amir. Oba's own name, Obadele, is an African one that in Swahili means "king." "Amir" means "prince" in Swahili. It is the perfect name. Amir is Oba's first son. Oba is king of our household, and Amir is one of our princes. Oba also wanted to leave a legacy for his father, so we gave Amir the middle name of Oliver, which is his dad's middle name.

One of the many things I love about Oba is that I know that he will make the best decisions for our family. Family means more to him than I can say, and he loves his family more than life. Admittedly, I'm stubborn and independent, but after I married him, I had to take a step back. The reason is that I wanted our boys to see that the man of the household must take charge of certain things, and I want my sons to develop that trait and personality. It's not for everybody, but it works for us. Yes, I share my thoughts with Oba, but it doesn't come down to "what he says, goes." Every time, our decisions are based on what is best for the family—that's our fundamental operating principle—and I think that is the best standard for us.

Even before we were married, Oba had been a constant presence in Monty's life. Oba adores Monty, and to Monty, Oba is Dad, or "Papa," as he is referred to.

The most important parent, biological or not, is the one who nurtures a child, seeing him through problems great and small every day.

Life was now more complete than I ever dreamed it could be. Somehow, after all the twists and turns our lives have taken—certainly with more to come—here we are as husband and wife, best friends, soul mates. He is the man God prepared me to be with—for the rest of my life.

The parts of my life I love the most now are the very ordinary ones:

being at home with our children, helping Monty with his school-work, reading bedtime stories, having birthday parties with hats and cake, and romping at the playground.

But I am getting ahead of myself. Life still had many painfully tough lessons in store for me.

CHAPTER 5

COMING CLEAN

I will never forget the day I finally plucked up the courage to admit the truth and give up the lie that had been burning up inside me for so many years. It was in September 2007. I woke up early and my mouth was dry. The day was balmy and warm, as is often the case in the middle of autumn in Austin, Texas, where Oba and I and the children had made our home.

I had been living a life stitched together from a textured weave of lies, every bit as meticulously fashioned as the $7,000 gowns I used to wear for magazine cover shoots. I couldn't live like this anymore. I couldn't sleep, I couldn't eat, I felt no joy.

I sat down with Oba and had a long, thoughtful discussion about what I was about to do. I have always been able to share my feelings and worries with him. He meets my emotional needs and ministers to me. He helped me see that we need to respond to our trials forthrightly and look them squarely in the face, with reliance on God. We also wanted to set a better example for our children by being honest.

We prayed together for strength and patience and for maintaining a positive, forward focus that is so much a part of our relationship. Finally, we prayed that this situation might somehow become a blessing for our family and that we would be given opportunities to touch other lives. After that, we sensed a peace that passes all understanding.

Later that evening I went to my desk, turned on my computer, and listened to its random clicks and whirs. I opened my email and from my address book, Oba and I gathered the names of close family and friends who would be the recipients of the letter I was about to write. Email might sound like an impersonal way to deliver a personal message, but it was the only way. I wouldn't have time to call everyone on our list and devote the time they'd each deserve. Further, I knew I couldn't get through a single call without crying.

I wanted our family and friends to know about the mistakes I had made. I wanted them to know that I would be pleading guilty to two counts of lying to federal agents. I wanted them to know that I had made a decision to break the law and that I was probably headed to jail. I wanted them to hear the truth from me and not from the media.

It was the hardest letter I've ever had to write, but it needed to be done. Finding the words was almost impossible. I knew that words couldn't even express how sorry I was for the untold harm I had done to our family and friends and how I let them down. I had to be honest to everyone and to myself. I had to apologize for all the heartache, misery, and stress I was causing everyone.

The peace I had felt earlier now gave way to pain. I kept thinking pain is supposed to teach us something. Things may break our hearts, but that pain is the price we pay for accepting a certain responsibility. I had to hang in there. I had to endure it. I had to remember that God wouldn't stop the pain, but He would help me get through it.

And so, staring at the blank computer screen, I began to write a long letter . . .

Dear family and close friends,

I hope this letter finds all of you well. I know some of you must be wondering where the pictures are that I so often attach to my emails. Unfortunately, this is a much different type of letter. I write this letter to all of you for a few reasons. The first is simply because I love you all. Some things will be happening in the next week that I want you all to know from me first. You deserve this because you have been there for me from the very beginning. You have supported me throughout the many struggles I have had in my life, and you continue to do so to this day. You deserve to hear about Marion from Marion and not from the USA Today *or* CNN.

The second reason is because I finally want to shed much baggage that has been tearing me down for a long time. I want to share with you all my humanness. I have made mistakes and bad

47

decisions, and I have carried a great amount of pain and hurt throughout my life. I want you all to understand that I had constructed, what I thought, was this impenetrable wall, to protect me from hurtful and harmful people and things. In doing this I, unfortunately, have distanced myself from loved ones and made myself impossible, at times, to connect with. I want you all to know that I sincerely apologize for this. One day soon, I hope you will understand the reason for me having such behavior. I am not trying to justify it, but simply want you all to have a better understanding of why I have done certain things in my life. Having said this, I realize the need to be up front and honest with you about several things that have transpired in my life. I will not candy coat the following statements, as I have tapped around the truth for too long.

I will get right to the crux of this letter. On October 5th, 2007, I plan to plead guilty to two counts of lying to federal agents.

In the letter I exposed my mistakes, my lying, and areas of personal trauma that most people would wish to conceal. Typing through tears, I continued . . .

I lied for a few reasons. I lied because I panicked. I lied to protect all that I had worked so very hard for in my life and career. And lastly, I lied to protect myself. It was an incredibly stupid thing to do. I made the decision to break the law and have to take full responsibility for doing so. All of this was after my attorneys had specifically told me several times how important it was to be totally truthful with the agents.

My emotions were overwhelming. I went through many boxes of tissues because writing the letter forced me to confront the many poor decisions I had made and how I had violated everyone's trust. Painfully, I wrote on . . .

The sentencing will be held in approximately three months, or sometime at the beginning of January. The sentencing guideline for an offense such as this is zero to six months in jail. Although it is extremely hard to fathom being away from my family for any length of time, I have to put the rest in God's hands and pray that this horrible chapter in my life be resolved as soon as possible. I wanted you to know this and not be surprised when you pick up the paper or turn on the computer within the next week. You deserve more than that.

The next several months will be very difficult for me and my family and all of you as well. With all of this happening, though, I want you to know that I already feel a huge relief being lifted as I will finally be able to tell the truth, as hard as it may be. I want to apologize to you all for all of this. I am sorry for putting you all through this after you have been there for me through everything. I want to apologize to you, in advance, for the questions that you will be asked about me and about your relationships with me. And lastly, I am sorry for disappointing you all, in so many ways. My intent was never to hurt any of you. Please keep me in your prayers.

    Love, Marion

As I wrote, I felt that my life had collapsed into debris, like a house after a tornado or a fire. Amid all the ruins, there were pieces and bits of my former life: pictures, trophies, medals—recognizable items that reminded me of the life I used to have. I was tempted to psychologically grab hold of those things and try to imagine ways to get that old life back. But that life was before the disaster. Those things are part of that huge pile of mess. I knew in my heart that the rubble had to be bulldozed away to make room to build a new foundation.

Often we are so preoccupied with what we have lost that we overlook what has been left. I knew there was something left to hold on to, though: the love of my husband, my children, and other family members. They reminded me that I was not left empty handed.

I believe in a God who can take our mistakes and move us from transition to transformation, a God who can take nothing and make the impossible possible. I wanted to use my mistakes to make my life stand for something positive and good, and I wanted everyone to know this. Trials are one of God's ways of forcing us to choose between blessing and bitterness. I also wanted my friends and family to know that I wasn't bitter.

I finished the letter at midnight, hoped my family would keep me in their prayers, and mouse-clicked the send button.

I felt a great sense of relief, as if an enormous burden had been lifted from my shoulders. The darkness comes, but then it goes. And as painful and as disturbing as it is, I am thankful that it doesn't last forever. The light does break.

I knew in my heart that I had done the right thing, and I knew in my soul that I'd never be the same again.

On October 5, 2007, I entered my guilty plea inside that packed U.S. District courtroom in White Plains to two counts of lying to federal prosecutors. Then I returned home to my family to await my sentencing a few months later.

The prosecutors recommended a sentence of zero to six months. My lawyers asked Judge Karas to limit the sentence to probation so that I would not be separated from my two young sons. I was still nursing Amir, who was just seven months old.

From the time a plea is entered to the sentencing, the probation department reviews the case. They interview people in your life. They accept letters sent from friends and family on your behalf. Mine came from my husband; my mother-in-law; my dear friend and former teammate, Melissa Johnson; a close friend of mine, Henry C. McKoy; and Sue Humphrey, head coach of the USA Women's 2004 Olympic Track and Field team. To all of you, I am forever grateful.

The probation department also investigates your finances, your education, and any prior offenses. Finally, they give the judge their recommendation for the sentence. The probation department's recommendation was probation, no jail time. Judges can do whatever they want, but I was told that most of the time, they lean toward the probation department's recommendation. So we were very hopeful going into the sentencing that I wasn't going to be sent to jail.

On January 11, 2008, I returned to the White Plains courtroom to hear my fate.

There, a dozen or so friends and family members were huddled in their seats. I hadn't seen some of these friends in years. There were even a few journalists who I knew were on my side. Oba, along with his mom, aunt, and sister were there. My mom, uncle, brother, and other close family members were also present. Although I was in a hostile environment, I had this incredible support system. I felt a sense of warmth, love, and peace. I thought to myself, "No matter what this judge says or does to me, I am going to be okay."

I asked the judge to be as merciful as a human being can be, so that I would not be separated from Monty and Amir. My voice quivered and I sobbed.

For what seemed like two hours, I listened to the judge recount my failings and transgressions.

Judge Karas said he wanted to send the message that lying to government investigators carried a stiff penalty.

"I want people to think twice before lying," Karas said. "I want to make them realize no one is above the law."

"Athletes in society have an elevated status," he said. "They entertain, they inspire, and perhaps most importantly, they serve as role models for kids around the world. When there is this widespread level of cheating, it sends all the wrong messages to those who follow these athletes' every move."

Then he pronounced my sentence.

Not swayed by my appeal to remain united with my sons, Judge Karas sentenced me to six months in federal prison, eight hundred hours of community service, and probation. Specifically, I was given six months for the first count of lying to federal investigators, stemming from the BALCO case, and two months for the second, to be served concurrently. That would be followed by two years of probation. I was ordered to surrender March 11 to begin my prison term.

After the judge declared the sentence, I remember looking to my right and left—I had an attorney on each side—then I turned and looked back at Oba. We were both dumbfounded. Six months in jail? Did we hear that right?

Yes, the judge had said "six months," and we were shocked.

After the sentencing, I hugged Oba, buried my face in his shoulder, and cried.

I then ventured outside to say a few words: "As I'm sure everyone can imagine, I'm extremely disappointed today. I respect the judge's orders. I truly hope that people will learn from my mistakes. But as I stood in front of all of you for years in victory, I stand in front of you today for what is right."

I had a chance to pay heartfelt thanks to everyone who had supported me. I said my goodbyes, with hugs, handshakes, and a final whispered few words.

It began to drizzle as we drove away from the courthouse. The drizzle gave way to a downpour. The rain fell in torrents, and a terrible storm rolled in. It was a physical storm, but there was an emotional storm inside my heart at the same time. I knew I had to put my trust in the One who is able to speak peace to the storm, so I could stand tall and not be terrorized by the torrent.

In a sad end to what seemed like a storybook career, I immediately gave back the three gold medals and two bronzes I'd won at the Games in 2000. I gave the medals to a representative of USADA, who then handed them over to the USOC. My track and field records from September 2000 on were scrubbed from the books. I was now a convicted felon. I can't even vote.

All of these things, however, paled in comparison to seeing my husband, my mother, and other close family members cry over how I had shattered our life by breaking the law.

I began to pick up the pieces and set out to explore what could be made of what was left. I knew that if there was anything left, then it was enough to hold on to. For the next two months, while I awaited my departure, I absorbed myself in family life. I meticulously prepared to have my two precious little boys sent to live with Oba's parents in Barbados. I did not want Monty and Amir to know I was in prison, much less visit me there.

I filled out birthday and anniversary cards for my family and friends and asked a friend to mail each one while I was gone. I sent birthday presents to my in-laws for the boys before leaving for prison, including recordings of me, reading some of Monty and Amir's favorite children's stories and a DVD of me, singing "Happy Birthday" to each boy (Monty would turn five and Amir would turn one while I was in prison). I had to do four or five takes before I could sing the song without breaking down in tears. I made a digital photo album for Monty and recorded prayers and bedtime songs on his MP3 player. Oba and I went to Build-a-Bear and had talking bears made with our voices. I did not want my sons to forget me but to know that I was with them in their hearts every single day.

I did a difficult interview on *The Oprah Winfrey Show*, struggling to answer questions about my family, my mistakes, and my upcoming prison sentence. It was one of the most painful media experiences of my life.

I eventually learned that I would be incarcerated at Carswell Federal Prison in Fort Worth, Texas. I Googled Carswell and read prison blogs. What popped up were reports of abuse, injustice, medical neglect, rape, and other atrocities. Terrified, I started preparing for hell. Meanwhile, an onslaught of humiliating stories about me hit the media worldwide.

I even asked then-President Bush to commute my sentence. My request put me on a list of hundreds of convicted felons who have applied for pardons or sentence commutations. A pardon is an official act of forgiveness. It removes civil liabilities stemming from a criminal conviction. A commutation reduces or eliminates a person's sentence.

It was not to be.

By this time, I was also broke and sinking into debt. A year earlier, a bank had foreclosed on my former home in Chapel Hill, North Carolina, and I had about two thousand dollars to my name. We were living off the money Oba had earned from his sports endorsements.

Before long, I saw my children off to Barbados, said tearful good-byes to my husband and my family, and prepared to surrender my normal life.

It was so painful that I can barely discuss it, even now.

One moment the sky of your life is clear; the next you can be buffeted, beaten, and tossed about by strong winds and torrential rainstorms. Storms are like that. They often appear out of nowhere, disrupting our plans and leaving devastation in their wake. Life is rarely the same after storms have hit. Mine certainly wasn't. And the storm didn't pass for a long time.

CHAPTER 6

CARSWELL

Raindrops fell from an ominous sky that hung over Austin on March 5, 2008, as Oba and I began our three-hour drive to Carswell Federal Prison in Fort Worth. Normally, during a long drive, we listen to audio books along the way. Oba prefers to start them as soon as we get in the car, whereas I like to settle into our driving rhythm before pressing play.

But that particular morning, I wanted to listen to the audio books right away. I think in some ways this was simply to have something else occupying our minds so that we would not have to think about the immediate future.

It usually takes us awhile to get through an audio book since we tend to pause it and talk about the characters. We also make bets on how the plot of the book will resolve. But today was different. For the most part, we silently listened as the narrator read the story; we hardly spoke.

But from time to time, I would reiterate all the things that I wanted him to remember to take care of while I was gone—things that I had probably told him a thousand times before. Oba would simply reply "okay" to most of them. He knew I just wanted to make sure that he and the boys were well taken care of during my absence. Twice we pulled over to gas stations because I felt a little queasy in my stomach.

After we got back on to the freeway, we spotted a sign for a donut shop. We both have a particular weakness for good donuts. Many mornings, after dropping Monty off at school, I'd end up at the donut shop around the corner from our house and return home with one or two. I had a feeling I wouldn't be eating donuts for a long time, so we swung into the parking lot. Oba went into the shop to get the donuts.

While I was waiting for Oba to return, one of my attorneys called to alert us that the media had gotten wind that I was self-surrendering today, and they might be waiting for us when we arrived at Carswell. This news did not surprise me at all. I was used to confidential, sensitive material leaking to the press, especially when it had anything to do with me.

A few minutes later, Oba returned to the car with half a dozen hot donuts in one hand and a caramel frappacino in the other, one of my favorite drinks. After hitting the road again, we stuffed the donuts down in seconds. Oba slept and I drove. While I drove, I prayed, and I prayed hard.

Two hours into the trip, I noticed a rainbow arching gracefully over the horizon. For me, a rainbow is all about divine promises.

The rainbow, after all, follows the storm. It is a promise, yes, a covenant, that I can trust God to be faithful during difficult times and know that He does not forget his own—ever. I smiled to myself and knew that although a judge had sentenced me, God had brought me to this place for a reason. I felt calm and at peace.

We weren't far from Carswell when we stopped at a post office. I mailed myself a few packages that I would receive while in prison— a tip I learned in a chat room while doing online research into the prison system. This act was the one last thing I wanted to do with my freedom before it was snatched from me.

As we resumed our drive to Carswell, our GPS unit led us to a dead-end road. From the Internet, I learned that Carswell would not show up officially on MapQuest or GPS units, most likely because it is located on a military base. Oba and I debated whether or not to continue. The GPS assured us that we were on the right path, so we drove ahead anyway, only to find ourselves bumping along a golf cart road. We sat there for a second, looked at each other, glanced at the GPS unit, and laughed. It was the only laugh we shared all morning. We turned around and found ourselves at a major intersection. We didn't know whether to turn right or left, so we flipped a coin and ended up going left. It was the right direction, and we arrived at Carswell a few minutes before 10 a.m.

We pulled up to the prison, officially known as The Federal Medical Center, Carswell (FMC, Carswell), just outside Fort Worth. It houses six hundred to seven hundred female offenders, some of whom have critical medical or psychiatric needs. They are as old as eighty-six and as young as eighteen and hail from every ethnic, social, and economic class—most of them having been convicted of white-collar or drug-related crimes. The prison is accessible only through the Naval Air Station Fort Worth, Joint Reserve Base, formerly known as Carswell Air Force Base.

The base has an interesting history. It was named after Medal of Honor recipient Horace S. Carswell, Jr. He died while crash-landing in the South China Sea after trying to save a crew member whose parachute had been destroyed by flak. In 1954, the Air Force base was prominently featured and used as a filming location in the movie *Strategic Air Command* starring James Stewart and June Allyson. On November 22, 1963, President John F. Kennedy and first lady Jacqueline Kennedy left a breakfast of the Fort Worth Chamber of Commerce and went by motorcade to Carswell Air Force Base for the thirteen-minute flight to Dallas's Love Field on Air Force One.

As Oba and I neared the base, before us loomed a compound of faceless whitish-gray, block-like buildings. There was a huge American flag waving atop a tall white pole like you see in the front of most government buildings. The prison was rimmed by acres of looped, razor-wire fencing.

At the front gate, two officers were waiting for us. After checking Oba's ID, one of the officers instructed us to follow two men in a gold GMC truck waiting to escort us inside. As we drove through the compound, we noticed an assortment of retired war planes and helicopters lining the roadsides.

Carswell opened as a hospital/prison for women in June 1994 after the Bureau of Prisons (BOP) closed its women's hospital in Lexington, Kentucky. A scathing government report singled out the Lexington hospital's care as being outrageously bad. Today, Carswell serves as the only medical and psychiatric referral center for women who have been convicted of a federal crime. One of its better-known inmates was Lynette "Squeaky" Fromme, the Charles Manson follower convicted of trying to assassinate President Gerald Ford. Currently serving time at Carswell is Wanda Barzee, who was convicted of kidnapping and unlawful transportation in the Elizabeth Smart abduction.

Carswell is a medium-security prison, but it has a reputation of being notoriously harrowing. Accusations of gross medical neglect, rape by prison guards, and toxic exposures have been reported by the media. In 1999, for example, a woman almost died from congestive heart failure after a physician's assistant diagnosed her severe chest pain as a urinary tract infection. That same year, a maintenance worker was totally disabled after days of exposure to lead dust from working there. In 2000, a woman died from brain cancer that was never properly treated.

Since 1997, seven men, including two chaplains, a counselor, and two gynecologists, have been convicted of rape or other sexual offenses against women there (another was fired for sexual misconduct but never brought to trial).

I was about to become a prisoner of this place, and I had no idea what to expect of prison life, except what I had seen on TV. I would be housed in a tiny room, living with women who had been there before, who knew the system, who knew how to work the guards. But I knew nothing. I kept thinking, *I have to get through this. I have to survive.*

The guards told us that Oba could not accompany me into the lobby where I would surrender.

Oba and I said painful good-byes in the prison parking lot. We spoke a few words of promise and encouragement to each other. We hugged and kissed one last time, both of us choking back our tears. "I love you!" He held me tightly and said he loved me too. As he left, I felt alone and scared.

I walked to a waiting truck where there were two prison officials. One was a large bulky man in his early fifties, the other much slimmer and younger. I buckled myself into the back seat. I had with me the few items I was allowed to bring: an inexpensive watch, my wedding band, small silver stud earrings, and my Bible. We drove up to a building where I would be "processed."

In three more steps, I was clutching the handles of the doors to a new world. I walked into the prison lobby and announced to a blank-faced woman in uniform, "I'm Marion Jones-Thompson, and I'm here to turn myself in."

She telephoned someone, then told me to have a seat.

Finally, another uniformed woman appeared and motioned me to follow her. She shuffled down the stark corridor with a zombie-like gait. As I passed down the hall, a few guards whispered to me that I would be okay.

But reality set in as soon as I was processed at Carswell, where the indignities began promptly. I was told to strip naked and cough—the idea being that any contraband I might be hiding inside me would tumble out. I told myself not to take any of this personally, but it was hard not to feel violated and persecuted. Many of the guards and inmates stared at me; they knew I was famous. I had to stay on my toes and trust no one. I reminded myself that I would get through this by becoming invisible: I would not act superior or scared. I vowed to follow orders and not rock the boat.

Over the next few days, I underwent a series of medical tests (for tuberculosis and HIV). I was issued three pairs of work pants, work shirts, five pairs of socks, four green T-shirts, one pair of pajamas, three bras, one sports bra, and six pairs of "Granny" panties. I was also given a pair of steel-toed boots, four towels, and two washcloths. All of the items had been used before except for the socks and underwear. I was given a hygiene pack that included a comb, deodorant, soap, toothpaste and toothbrush, as well as shampoo and conditioner. They also gave me a cup full of laundry detergent to get started. Officially, I was now nothing more than a number: Federal Inmate Number 84868-054.

From researching the prison system, I learned that it was a good idea to find a job before I was assigned one. I navigated my way over to the Education Department and filled out a "call out" form, indicating the particular prison job assignments in which I was interested.

I was told I could conduct an essay class for inmates working on their GEDs. Many of the women prisoners were Hispanic and didn't speak English, yet they had to be able to write a paragraph in English in order to pass the test. I was excited by the idea that I could give them some help so they could move on with their lives. Writing is a skill, and that's why it can be so helpful to prisoners. Anything they can master makes them more sure of themselves and more capable of doing well in the world.

"You'll have to have your transcripts sent to us," said one of the corrections officers in the Education Department.

"No problem," I said. "I'll get in touch with my college and have them forward my transcripts to you."

The officer looked at me like I was an idiot.

"Not your college transcripts, your high school transcripts," she said sternly.

I couldn't believe it. Whoever needs high school transcripts as verification of anything? If you're going to teach, it would seem that college transcripts would be appropriate, if not superior, credentials. I learned right away that prison operated on a different set of rules.

Besides some GED courses, the only programs Carswell offered for inmates were a keyboarding course that used outdated software, a cosmetology course, and some yoga classes. It was sad for me to see all the inmates sitting or walking around Carswell so idle and bored, when they could have been educating themselves, had there been more opportunities to do so.

Eventually, I was assigned to the kitchen to work as a baker. While I love anything drenched in sugar, I hate cooking and baking. You'd never drive by my house and smell the aroma of cookies, cake, or bread. I'd be earning thirteen cents an hour as a baker. God does have a sense of humor, for sure.

That first day, I explored the prison a bit. The Recreation Department had a treadmill, a stair-climbing machine, and other equipment. It was old but otherwise in good working condition.

Then I found the track. Unlike the hundreds of high-tech, rubberized tracks I'd been on, this one was made with gravel. But it was located right next to sparkling Lake Worth. I started running. As I circled the track, I noticed dozens of inmates standing on a balcony and at the windows of the cafeteria, watching me. For more than two hours, I ran repeats of 200-meter sprints, a track event in which I had won a gold medal.

Then I headed to my new home: an old Motel 6 that had been swallowed up by the prison and converted to a dormitory where approximately 275 women were housed. The corridors exuded a time-worn gloom, with long stretches of dingy walls. Certain odors went all the way down to the core of my memory: Carswell smelled like a sweaty locker room that somehow ended up inside a public restroom in dire need of cleaning.

My room had two metal bunk beds and a single bed, each with a thin mattress on top, along with a sheet and pillow and two blankets. The mattress was old and soiled; I wouldn't let my chow Izzy sleep on such a thing. I wondered what living organisms were lurking inside it, probably millions of microscopic dust mites munching microscopic skin flakes shed by sleepers. I asked to have my mattress sanitized, but my request fell on closed ears. I was given the okay to drag it outside and beat it with a broom to get the dust off.

The heating and air conditioning unit kept me awake almost every night. One minute it was hot, and the next it was cold. Unfortunately, my bunk was right next to the unit and window, so I got the draft from the window, the fumes when the heat kicked in, as well as the cold air when the AC switched over.

Eventually, I figured out how to solve these problems so I could sleep. I wore my flannel underwear under a T-shirt. I wore sweat pants rather than the flimsy prison-issued pajama bottoms. I put on my thick socks and wore them to bed.

I also positioned myself on the side of the bed furthest from the AC unit. Lastly, I'd pull one of the blankets up to my shoulders. I'd fold the other blanket and drape it over my head. But I had to keep at least one body part visible at night so that during the nightly body count, the guard wouldn't have to lift my covers and shine a flashlight in my eyes to make sure that I hadn't escaped.

As for that body count at night, I never got used to it. I always jumped when they opened the door. The worst part was when some of the more inconsiderate guards slammed the doors after they left and woke us up unnecessarily.

As a new inmate, I had to attend an orientation meeting, where we were allowed to ask questions. So, naturally, I spoke up. I wanted to know whether the rooms we lived in had ever been inspected for asbestos or mold. From the first day I arrived, I noticed what appeared to be mold in the bathroom. In addition, I knew that these buildings were old and probably built during the time when asbestos was a commonly used building material. The prison official confirmed that there was indeed asbestos in these buildings but not the type that crumbles, which is the deadly kind. Although she said that the buildings had been tested and approved, I was not convinced by her answers, but I felt helpless to do anything about it.

I had a few measures of relief: For instance, there was the track with its wonderful view of the lake and the outdoor recreation yard nearby. On my endless days of exercise, I'd cherish the delicately colored streaks of dawn. Even the tiny patches of grass on the lawns or ripples on the lake were, for me, pleasing to look at.

I also learned a new sport in prison—Hacky Sack—in which you kick a mini soccer-type ball around in a circle of people. The goal is to kick it without letting it hit the ground or using your hands. I was invited to play one day, and the players taught me how to play acceptably well. The first time, I spent an hour outside playing with them and thoroughly enjoyed myself. But I nearly ripped my Achilles tendon one time trying to get the ball. I decided to slow it down a bit.

After a couple of weeks in prison, the other inmates got used to me. There wasn't much gawking, and I was down to only one autograph seeker a day. I began to feel like a "normal inmate," whatever that is. Whoever thinks they would ever be saying that? I certainly never had. My roommates even shared with me how much they respected the way I came to prison with a smile, a positive attitude, and my head held high.

There was a church service every Saturday night. The first time I attended, I was disappointed to see such poor attendance. My roommates guessed that about 10 percent or less of the Carswell population went to church. This got me thinking about starting a Bible study. I knew God had put me here for a reason. Could that be it? Could I be a messenger? Aren't we all messengers if we're doing right by God?

Unfortunately, I found out that the inmates had tried to have Bible studies, but the guards put an end to them. If inmates congregated, the guards feared they might be conspiring against the prison.

My first and only holiday in prison was Easter, and I volunteered to be in an Easter play. Ironically, I got to play the part of a judge: Caiaphas, the Jerusalem high priest who presided over the trial of Jesus. According to the Gospels, Jesus was arrested at night after being betrayed by Judas and taken under the cover of darkness to a secret trial before Caiaphas. In Matthew, Caiaphas asks Jesus: "Tell us if you are the Christ, the Son of God" (Matthew 26:63 NIV). Jesus answers in no uncertain terms, "Yes, it is as you say" (Matthew 26:64 NIV).

At the time, this was considered blasphemy, a crime punishable by death. Caiaphas was the leader of the religious group called the Sadducees, who were on good terms with Rome at the time. He hated Jesus because He taught a message that the Sadducees could not accept. And so Caiaphas pressured Pilate to put Jesus to death. Caiaphas later conspired to cover up the resurrection.

My role in the play got me thinking about all of this. There are so many people in this world, like Caiaphas, who are closed to the truth, even to the truth of God. I guess they think it will cost them too much to believe in Christ. He is on trial in so many human hearts, even today.

The Easter service was uplifting. I was so glad that I decided to skip my workout to attend. The Word of God renewed my spirit and opened the eyes and hearts of eight women who decided that their future was more important than their past.

In the sermon, I was reminded that Jesus told his disciples over and over again that he was going to die and that in three days he would be raised from the dead. And in order to validate his claim, he would need to be seen by some witnesses after he was raised from the dead. Who would be the first to behold the face of the resurrected Lord? Who would be the first to witness the results of the greatest event in human history?

It turned out to be a woman, Mary Magdalene, out of whom Jesus had cast seven demons. She was a woman with a past, a woman with bondage in her life. I knew if Jesus could deliver Mary Magdalene who had seven demons, He could deliver me from my past. My past wasn't going to stop me from seeing God in my life. I may have gone through some terrible things in my past, but I knew that the Lord was willing to forgive me, reveal himself to me, and give me another chance.

Monty had also performed in an Easter play in Barbados. I called to find out how it went. Oba's mom told me about how well Monty had recited his lines. He had shown no signs of stage fright. In fact, he was so good that the audience asked him to recite his part again. I was so proud of him. I would have loved to have been in the front row, cheering him on.

In prison, we'd arise between 4:30 and 5:30 a.m. to shower and grab breakfast before we reported for our work shift. Lunch was anywhere from 11:30 a.m. to 1:00 p.m. If I wasn't working, I'd be free to go outside and enjoy the weather or do some workouts in the recreation area. Next would be dinner, an hour or two of free time in the evening, and bedtime.

Our days were extremely regimented; we were counted several times by guards changing shifts so they could make sure we were present and alive. There was very little decent food or anything even remotely fresh served in jail. Occasionally, there would be fresh fruit that I'd take back to my room. But it immediately attracted little flies so I had to toss it out. The meat looked like dog food. I once saw a cockroach crawl out of a bread pan and skitter for cover.

Once a week, we were allowed to go to the commissary, the prison store. Since we couldn't carry cash, money we earned or money deposited by friends or relatives went into a fund that we could use to buy items in the commissary. Our monthly spending limit was three hundred dollars. One of the inmates hadn't touched money in so long that she wasn't sure whether she knew the difference between a dime and quarter. "After I'm released, I'm going to look like a fool if I have to go into a store and count out money to buy something," she told me. "I don't know if I can deal with the embarrassment."

The line to get into the commissary was always very long; those with rooms closest to the commissary were usually first to enter. If you were at the end of the line, it might take two hours to actually get inside. My room was farther away and that put me at a disadvantage, so I usually ran.

"Jones, you're running so fast," quipped a guard, "that I ought to give you a speeding ticket."

I felt sorry for some of the older and disabled ladies who couldn't get there fast enough and were always relegated to the back of the line. The whole system was antiquated and demeaning.

We could use email in prison but were charged five cents a minute. The time was deducted from our commissary accounts. We couldn't be online for more than thirty minutes at a time. Unless I limited myself to checking email once in the morning and once in the evening, I'd be broke by the second week in each month.

One day, some of the prison guards arrested a television film crew that was trying to jump the fence. Some of my fellow inmates figured maybe it had something to do with me. I thought to myself that it was unfortunate that even on a military base, my security and privacy were compromised.

Another time, the warden sent out an email to everyone on the base asking that, when they were driving by the track and soccer fields, to not talk to me, photograph me, or ask me for autographs. One of my roommates shared this information with me after she returned from work. I didn't doubt her veracity, since shortly afterwards, the prison put up signs that read: "No Standing, No Stopping, No Photographing, and No Communicating with Inmates." It was sad to me how the Bureau of Prisons had money to spend on a dozen or so signs around the prison but claimed that there was no money in the budget for proper medical care or educational programs.

I called Monty and Amir every other night. Monty was always wonderfully talkative and energetic.

"Mama, I have something to tell you," he said one night, "but it's a secret."

"You don't have to tell me then," I said.

"But I want to!" He was adamant. I could just picture him, stomping his little feet.

"Okay, certainly you can tell me."

His voice dropped to a whisper. "Me and Amir are going to buy you a diamond ring for your birthday!"

I was overcome with emotion and tears began to fall. "That would be the second best gift ever. The first best would be the biggest hug from my three guys."

Another time, Monty cried on the phone because he missed me a lot. I tried to be tough and hold back tears, but I soon began to cry as well. This was the first time I had heard him cry. Up until that moment, he seemed so jovial and carefree. I wanted so much to tell him that I was coming over to see him and that we would snuggle in bed. I wanted him to hear in my voice the amount of unconditional love I have for him and Amir. I finally convinced him to stop sniffling and crying so that I could say prayers and sing to him. He kissed the phone and we said our good nights. I was heartbroken.

Once, when I talked to my mother-in-law, she told me that Amir took what she thought was his first step. I was devastated to miss it but overjoyed that he was on the move. I wanted so much to be there for those happy times. It's moments like those—your child's first steps or their first word—precious moments that you never get back again. Once you've missed them, that's it.

I knew I needed to tell my children I loved them and tell them as often as I could. I kissed their pictures every night before I went to bed. If you spend one night in prison, you will appreciate everything you have waiting for you on the outside. I can certainly look back on things that have occurred in my life, and I can find reasons to grumble, gripe, and complain. But when I put them on the scale of life and weigh out the negative things against the good things, the good things always outweigh the bad.

What kept me going in prison were Oba's regular visits. He came to Carswell every weekend and would often stay through Monday night, which at the prison were our "date nights." Without his love and support, I would have lived a lonely existence. Every time I saw him, my eyes lit up and my heart skipped beats. His whisper of, "I love you, baby" in my ear were the sweetest words a woman could hear.

We would chat about general topics while we stole loving glances and an occasional furtive touch. Human contact is illegal in prison, even during visitations with relatives. The exception is with your children. Even so, my visits with him allowed me to stay focused on the important things in life—our faith, our family, and our love. He was—and is—my rock.

Oba spent his thirty-second birthday visiting me at Carswell. Imagine, celebrating a special occasion visiting your spouse in prison. What a marvelous gift, right?

When I cried during his visits, it was because I am so thankful that God had sent him into my life. We'd say our goodbyes, and then I'd watch him walk out the door.

There were times, usually late at night when things finally began to quiet down, that I'd lay on my bunk and wonder, "How could all the accumulated success of my athletic life—the glory, the money, the adoration—so quickly disappear?" That is a pretty silly question; obviously the answer is that I broke the law.

Then from somewhere the thought would come, "Hold it. For all you have lost, there is still so much remaining that is worthy of love. You have a family who needs you and a life to be fulfilled."

And so, I forced myself to settle in as best I could. Many times, I took a deep breath and prayed that, whatever I was supposed to learn, I would learn it well. My belief that I was doing the right thing buoyed my morale.

While imprisoned, I focused more on God and found comfort in prayer and Scripture. In despair, the natural tendency is to give up. Either we can give up on God, or we can hold to Him. I chose to hold on.

CHAPTER 7

FAITH AND SURVIVAL

At Carswell, every day was a struggle for survival. The monotony of the daily round was enough to deaden the spirit. The relentless noise—shouting conversations, clanging doors, blowing fans, and flushing toilets—allowed few occasions for quiet and rest. Mail call could be a heaven or a hell for a woman, depending on whether she got mail. Practically every conversation was eavesdropped upon. Regular pat-down searches, strip searches, and room searches occurred in the endless hunt for contraband. Life there was like stepping out of the real world into some sort of frozen limbo state.

After first arriving at Carswell, I was nervous about meeting my roommates, as well as other inmates. I expected to hear stories of innocence and bitterness and of the terrors of living behind bars. What I experienced instead was a life-altering glimpse into the lives of many women who had, perhaps, made the wrong choices in life, but who had taken full responsibility for those choices and were trying desperately to make the best of a bad situation. Ironically, I found much of my strength to survive in several of the female inmates I met. They were like plants that bend toward the light, no matter how dim the room. It was from them that I learned how to thrive in the darkness of uncertainty and crisis.

For those who believe that all female offenders are superviolent or uneducated or indifferent to their circumstances, these women beg to differ. While they have seen more in their lives than most of us ever will, they also have learned more about themselves and the world than most people do in a lifetime. Many were an inspiration to me— they were making the best of a bleak-but-not-hopeless life in prison.

The sentences imposed on many of the women were startling in their harshness. Many were incarcerated for years for seemingly petty offenses like cheating once on their taxes or unknowingly committing mail fraud. It makes you angry but also sympathetic, because we have the feeling that any of us, in such a position, might have succumbed to the same temptation.

"The system isn't always fair. There are lots of rules and regulations, and those who break the rules cause trouble for all. When something happens, most of us get punished. There isn't much individuality. But I've learned I can survive prison, mostly by relying on myself and my own inner resources."

That statement came from one of my roommates, Victoria, forty-two, a mother of two, who, oddly enough, is married to a state trooper. But it could apply to any of the women who made an impression on me: Laura, a kind, perky grandmother who was finishing a sixteen- ·

year sentence for a crack cocaine offense; Tonja, a heavyset black woman, who spoke of her former life as a counterfeiter and identity thief with equal parts candor and regret; Nancy, a quiet woman with a nervous manner who was the mother of twin boys; Kori, a talkative black woman with a heart of gold; another cellmate, Beth, sixty-four, a bow-legged woman and former bank president who was serving five years for some type of fraud; and Janice, a tiny, black woman in her mid forties from the Virgin Islands.

I don't know their whole stories, but after getting to know them on a personal level, I feel that not everyone who commits a crime is a criminal. Behind the walls of Carswell are mothers, daughters, wives, friends, and neighbors—all persons made in the divine image of God who, like the rest of us, have distorted that image, made mistakes, and long for love, reconciliation, and purpose.

I doubt that any of these inmates' crimes made the front page. Yet these were only seven of the hundreds of female inmates at Carswell, part of a national trend that has seen the women's prison population climb. According to the Women's Prison Association, the female prison population grew by 832 percent from 1977 to 2007. The male prison population grew by 416 percent during the same period. Today, more than 200,000 women are in prison and jail in the United States.

A lot of the women I met at Carswell fit the following profile: white women who were nonviolent drug-related offenders, serving an average sentence of nine years. Specifically, 64 percent were white,

33 percent black, and the rest, American Indian or Asian. Of the white population, 22 percent were of Hispanic descent. This profile pretty well matches the female inmate breakdown of prisoners nationwide, according to the most recent statistics from the Bureau of Prisons.

What goes on behind the walls of the prison is a mirror in many ways of what happens in society, and that includes prejudice and bigotry. At Carswell, there was an itchy racial tension among white, black, and Hispanic prisoners and rarely any mingling of ethnicities. The racial incidents were primarily Hispanics going after blacks. I was standing in line one day, waiting to talk to a corrections officer, when a young Hispanic girl began speaking in Spanish to a friend of hers. Unaware that I speak and understand Spanish, they were talking about a black roommate whom they hated. They were conspiring to give her problems, such as bumping her in the commissary line and stepping on her fingers whenever she climbed down from her top bunk. I couldn't resist speaking up. In Spanish, I told them that I could not stand around and let them disrespect anyone. They just rolled their eyes.

Normally though, I got along with the Hispanic ladies. Carswell has a Spanish TV room. The first time I walked in to get some hot water, some of the women glared at me, showing the fierceness of cornered forest animals.

I spoke in Spanish to them, and the ice broke. From then on, they always invited me for dinner whenever they cooked Mexican food.

Had a riot broken out at Carswell, I wouldn't have been surprised. Prison, with its racial animosities, is a breeding ground for violence. Racial conflict, lying just beneath the surface of the day's slow routine, can be ignited by a word, a look, or a stumble. It's a funny thing about prisons: You lock people up away from society, but they take the problems of society with them.

All of my roommates, except for one, were white. In the beginning, I associated mostly with these white women. Some of the black inmates made assumptions about me because of it. But once they got to know me, they saw me as just me. For as long as I can remember, I've never been one to befriend only one group or ethnicity. I always act the same around all people, and I have many friends from all races, cultures, and walks of life. So, the racial division at Carswell troubled me.

The importance of getting along with my roommates reminded me of a relay. Track is partly a team sport. When you're in an individual event like the 100-meter or 200-meter dash, you're on your own. But when you're in a relay, you're really depending on your teammates. That's the thing about a relay; you have to have chemistry. You have to get along and know each other's tendencies and what the other person is thinking before they even think it. You need to have some kind of bond, no matter what race or background you come from.

A small percentage of the women at Carswell were not U.S. citizens and faced deportation at the completion of their sentences. About 8 percent were serving terms of twenty or more years. According to the most recent data I could find from Carswell, most were imprisoned for drug offenses (62 percent); the rest for extortion, bribery, and fraud (about 8 percent); weapons, explosives, and arson (7.6 percent); and robbery (6.4 percent).

So how did these women survive in such isolation with so few privileges? As I did, most set their sights on a goal—their freedom, their children, and their families.

"I've always had one aim, one goal, and that's my freedom," said Laura, who showed me around my first day. Laura was being released the very next day (March 8) after serving sixteen years. During her sentence, she saved her ten cents an hour and accumulated more than a thousand dollars in her savings account—money she was allowed to take home with her. She also survived two breast cancer scares and the removal of an eight-inch cyst from her body.

"I just want to press forward, be positive. I won't take any bitterness out there with me. I want to take the lessons I've learned and, you know, grow from this experience."

During her time, Laura earned the trust and respect of every guard and staff member at Carswell. She was placed in charge of accompanying inmates who needed medical care to their medical appointments outside the prison. She also helped with inmate orientation. I appreciated her kindness so much on my first day that I wrote her a short note thanking her for her generosity and kindness to me. She told me that of all the inmates she'd met in sixteen years, I was the only one who ever thanked her in writing.

Upon her release, Laura jumped into the car with her daughter, took the wheel, honked the horn, and blasted the radio as she drove past the buildings that had housed her for sixteen years. She would finally be able to see her fifteen grandbabies and two great grandbabies, plus make a surprise visit to her son, who, sadly, was in jail. Laura had not seen him since she entered Carswell in 1992.

Her story brought me to tears. I cried because I was happy for her release and the demonstration of God's extraordinary power in people's lives.

Victoria, who slept in the bunk beneath mine, took me under her wing from the beginning and guided me through the do's and don'ts of prison life. "I don't have that many fears about being here," she said. "I've gotten used to it. I know my place. I know what I need to do."

Victoria was a former model and CFO of a company. Her skin was the color of watery cream, and her eyes were dark and penetrating.

Victoria's husband and children were waiting for her "on the outside"—two daughters, a twenty-one-year-old and a thirteen-year-old.

Victoria was often very sad. Her story, which she told in a tumble of words, revealed the source of her sadness.

"I've missed a lot, and I feel so guilty for the toll that my actions have taken on my family," she said, rocking back and forth on her bunk and fingering a photograph of her family. Her voice trailed off for a moment and tears clouded her eyes.

"My children are precious to me, and I have them on my mind all the time. They know the real me. I miss them so much."

I hugged her and we both cried for a bit. I wanted her to know that she wasn't alone in the sadness of separation. I understood. When mothers are sentenced to time behind bars, our children are condemned to serve out our terms in the outside world without us. The razor-barbed wire, the armed guards, and the locks and doors mark the border between our separate worlds.

Victoria was always doing favors for me. One time, Oba was eight minutes too late for visiting hours and was barred from entering the prison. I got worried because I was expecting him and didn't know what to think. Victoria called her husband, gave him Oba's cell phone number "in code," and asked him to call my husband to make sure he was okay. Victoria had to speak in a special code because making a call for someone else in prison is strictly prohibited. She returned to our room and wrote on a piece of paper that Oba would come tomorrow. I was so relieved to finally get word that Oba was okay.

Victoria was among the most creative and talented women at Carswell. She could crochet an entire blanket in just week. She taught me how to crochet, although I have since sadly forgotten how to do it.

Many women come out of prison with poor prospects for jobs or education. A woman is released and expected to make a living, support herself and her children, and be a productive member of society with little help in the way of education or job-skills training, along with the stigma of having been in prison. What happens to them once they leave is often a mystery. Many return to their hometowns, only to get swallowed up in the lifestyle that got them incarcerated in the first place. Many eventually land back in prison.

I don't think this will happen to Nancy, though. Nancy was the mother of twenty-four-year-old twin boys and two other children, one sixteen and the other twelve.

"All of us in prison are searching for the same thing—a stronger sense of ourselves," she said.

The daily indignities of prison life did not stop Nancy from finding it. She enrolled in the few classes that were available so that she will have some kind of employable skill after she is released. She planned to become a dental hygienist. Her spirit of preparation was her ticket to self-respect and the surest road to independence outside Carswell. Whether a woman becomes successful outside the gates is mostly up to her.

A number of the women I met came from angry places. They were born into families where parents were alcoholics or used heroin, cocaine, or other drugs. Those parents usually did not get along well with each other, especially when they were drunk or high. Some of the women came from broken homes. Husbands, boyfriends, or fathers were abusive. Women were kicked or beaten by their mates' or fathers' fists. Many had been sexually abused.

You might find this odd, but despite the sadness, tragedies, and conditions we were forced to endure in Carswell, we did manage to find laughter. Of all the women I met at Carswell, Tonja was the funniest. Tonja, in prison for counterfeiting and identity theft, is a heavyset black woman with a wild, spiky corkscrewed mop of black hair. She wanted people to think she was nuts so that they would underestimate her. She was actually quite intelligent. Tonja had an unusual background for a prisoner. Apparently, she once appeared on Comedy Central. She told us jokes about falling into her aunt's coffin and a hundred other funny stories. I wasn't sure how long her sentence was, but I knew that her humor helped her endure. Doing time is hard. If you don't have a sense of humor, it's really tough to get through it.

I feared for Tonja, though. Every time she was released from prison, she'd head home. But before long, mired in her old fraud-and-crime ways, she'd land right back where she started. Tonja didn't believe in herself or her God-given talents enough to believe that her life could be any different.

One of my favorite women at Carswell was Kori, a sophisticated African-American woman. She walked so confidently every day around the track that I immediately gravitated toward her.

I could relate to Kori. She had made one bad decision—to commit mail fraud. It was innocent, almost. Kori had managed an apartment complex and someone overpaid her. She decided to use the extra money to help out her ailing father, with every intention of paying it back. She sent some correspondence regarding all of this through the mail, which counts as a felony. Kori was sentenced to

My newborn pic, birth date:
October 12, 1975

First birthday, October 12, 1976

Left: First participation in an organized
sport—T-ball, 6 years old, 1981
Right: Enjoying T-ball as a little girl,
8 years old, 1983

Top Right: Great photo op, but it was never really my thing!; *Top Left:* Ballet lessons, 7 years old, 1982; *Bottom Left:* On a school trip to the zoo in California, 9 years old, 1984; *Bottom Right:* Byron Scott Basketball Camp in California, 1986

Top Left: Rio Mesa High School, 13 years old, 1989; *Top Right:* Thousand Oaks High School, 1992; *Bottom Left:* Rio Mesa High School, 1990; *Bottom Right:* Thousand Oaks High School graduation, 17 years old, 1993

University of North
Carolina basketball, my
freshman year, 1994
*(Courtesy of UNC Athletics
Communications)*

UNC basketball
*(Courtesy of UNC Athletics
Communications)*

The 2000 Olympics, 200-meter victory!

Left: My wedding day; *Right:* The last day I would see our boys before heading to Carswell, February 29, 2008 (From left to right: Oba, Monty, me, Amir)

Top: Carswell Federal Prison in Ft. Worth, Texas; *Middle:* A few of my friends and fellow inmates at Carswell waving good-bye to me as Oba and I drive away, August 19, 2008; *Bottom:* Oba picking me up from Carsell after my release, August 19, 2008

Me and Oba picking the boys up from the Austin airport after their return from Barbados, September 6, 2008 (From left to right: Oba, Amir, me, Monty)

Left: Proud big brothers of Eva-Marie, August 2009 (From left to right: Monty, Eva-Marie, Amir)
Right: My greatest treasures, March 26, 2010 (From left to right: Monty, Eva-Marie, Amir)
Bottom: My family, December 2009 (From left to right: Amir, Oba, me, Eva-Marie, Monty)

Top: New opportunities with the WNBA, 2010;
Middle: Playing for the Tulsa Shock, 2010;
Bottom: Talking with the kids at a WNBA Cares event

twenty-six months at Carswell. Like me, she expected probation, but got jail time instead.

Also like me, Kori had two small children, little girls. Every visitation, her husband Lorenzo dressed those girls up to come see Kori. They'd all sit together and count the days until Kori could come home. Lorenzo was a loving, sweet presence. We all loved him.

One afternoon after working out, I stopped to talk to Kori. She was sitting on the bleachers, crocheting a blanket for one of her daughters. We started joking about strip searches and how humiliating they could be. She shared with me a few of her experiences.

"After one of the visitations with my family, I was randomly chosen to be strip-searched. As I began removing my clothes, I remembered that I was on my period and was using a tampon. There I was, naked, waiting for the guards to tell me it was okay to put my clothes back on.

"Then one of the guards noticed the string hanging down from the tampon. She yanked the tampon out of me, saying it was prison policy to remove them. It was the most embarrassing moment of my life."

Passed from visitors to prisoners, tampons have been known to harbor drugs or other contraband. I am not sure how I would react or respond to this happening to me, but I prayed that it didn't.

When I watched Beth, one of my roommates, she was always in motion, despite her bowlegs and bad knees. A real fireball, she always had something to do: talking, writing, reading her Bible, or cleaning (her favorite). Beth was petrified of breaking prison rules and getting punished, so she was forever straightening up our room. Her family lived far away.

One day, she unreeled the litany of her unhappy prison life with an unsettling, twitchy anxiety.

"I don't get any visits," she confided to me. "You know, when you first come down here, you get a whole lot. Then once you're here for a while, they get farther and farther apart. I sometimes sit around and wonder if my family remembers who I am."

The first day I was at Carswell, Beth brought me hot chocolate and a honey bun from the cafeteria. She had been incarcerated for five years for a money-related crime while serving as vice-president of a bank in Kansas City.

We called her "Mrs. Beth" because we all looked up to her and respected her, as if she was our grandmother.

And in a way, she was. Mrs. Beth's most important trait was that she was a giver, and she mothered us all. She reminded me of the importance of giving to others, and that giving should never end. It is one of the reasons we should get up every day. When we help others, we take the focus off of ourselves. When I started looking outside myself and realized that people who are worse off than me have overcome and survived, I began to see new possibilities for my own life.

I got to thinking, too: There are so many honest organizations out there in need of volunteers to help with their day-to-day activities. Why can't the prison supply volunteers? Volunteering would certainly boost the morale of some of these women who already think they are less than human because of past abuses and experiences in their lives. I believe it's vital to teach these women that they can be productive members of society, and I don't think you can do that by forcing them to clean toilets. There was little encouragement or positive affirmation—few incentives to keep trying or strengthening self-worth.

When you're in prison, you can't live like you would if you were on the outside. Fortunately, we had a "hairdresser" to make life more bearable. Her name was Janice, a slight, light-skinned woman in her mid forties from the Virgin Islands. She reminded me of women from the islands—fresh-faced, robust, and sweet in nature.

Carswell had a hair salon of sorts on the premises. About the size of a small hotel room, it had a couple of old-style hair dryers and a sink. We'd go in there to hang out and talk, especially in the summer. The salon was air-conditioned, and we could escape the heat. Like any salon you go to, pieces of conversation floated into the air, as inmates, giddy as teenagers at the prospect of fussing with their looks, chatted away.

Janice worked here, alongside some other women. She loved pampering her fellow prisoners. You could get your hair done or nails painted or enjoy a pedicure—as long as you supplied the shampoo, perm, hair coloring, or nail polish, which could be obtained from the commissary. You paid for your hairdos or manicures with items your stylist wanted from the commissary.

The salon was more important than you might think. To me, it was a symbol of the entire process of dignity and self-worth so greatly needed in prison. You could go there to pretty up and then come out feeling good about yourself.

For me, I couldn't control what clothes I put on, but I did have control over my hair, so I took pride in getting it done every weekend right before Oba's visit.

Janice was jailed over an immigration offense. That she was a first-time offender didn't matter much. She had been found guilty and given the maximum sentence of ten years because she hadn't been willing to snitch on a friend. By the time I met her, she was in the seventh year of her incarceration.

Janice lived in the room above me, so it was easy to get my hair done, and she did a wonderful job. My hair is long, so sometimes, I would let her just experiment with it. That way, she got a chance to play with long hair, and it was fun for her.

As Janice wrapped my hair one day, she told me, "I decided that when I get home, this is what I'm going to do—go into business and open a beauty school in Antigua where my father lives."

I so admired Janice and the others for their goals and dreams. They gave meaning and purpose to their lives. As Langston Hughes said, "Hold fast to dreams, for if dreams die, life is a broken-winged bird that cannot fly."

Most of these women were not paralyzed by their past nor stuck in their sorrow. They learned to let it go and move forward with hope. They taught me that our goal is to create the best life possible with what we have. Yes, we will face challenges, but if we press on, we will make it. The past is the past, and it doesn't have to dictate our future. We are in control of our destiny, and if we take the appropriate action steps to create our best future possible, we will create the life we want.

When I traveled the world as an athlete, I saw new people and new places, and not all of it was nice. I saw all different types of people who, like me, made all kinds of mistakes, but I still feel everybody has something good inside.

Every human being is so much more than the worst thing he or she has ever done. You have a culture of people who have been incarcerated because they've committed a crime, but there's always the possibility that they can turn around and do the right thing after they've made a mistake.

Each story I've shared here is a reminder to me of the ways, grand and small, that people hold on and keep going and push back against whatever darkness they have in their lives.

CHAPTER 8

THE PRISONS WE MAKE

The prison culture also includes guards and corrections officers. Some of them were sympathetic, empathetic, and caring, and others seemed filled with a desire to control and, too often, abuse the power they have over the lives of other people. In this chapter, I'll share with you a few in both categories.

One day, I got word that Counselor B wanted to see me. "Counselor" is another term for "corrections officer." In my opinion, they really do not "counsel" anyone. Other inmates had warned me to steer clear of this guy, that he was the meanest and rudest guard in the prison. Women prisoners would leave his office in tears. Victoria told me there were times that, after she handed him paperwork, he'd crumple it up right there and throw it on the ground. So I decided to proceed with caution.

I knocked on his door. I heard a deep "Yes." Counselor B then told me to enter and be seated. His hair was graying and his face pale. He didn't get up from his desk; he just sat there, like a toad basking on a rock. Country music played in the background and pictures of Marines were plastered all over his wall.

Counselor B recited the prison rules to me. His head stayed buried in the rule book and never once did he look me in the eye. He snarled that I should not give anyone autographs or pictures while in prison and was not to become friends with staff or inmates.

His tone of voice was so degrading, that it made the hair on my arms stand up. I might have committed a crime and made a mistake, but that doesn't give anyone the right to disrespect me. To this day, I don't know why he requested to see me, but I will never forget how he made me feel.

Another example of the unyielding power prison officials have over inmates' lives played out when I requested a transfer from kitchen duty to the recreation department. One of the reasons I wanted to transfer was Mr. Conrad, who supervised the kitchen where I worked. He had reddish wispy hair and a sneer on his face calibrated to foster disrespect. He called inmates names like "crackhead" and other derogatory terms. He yelled or barked orders and wouldn't know the words "thank you" or "good morning" if they walked up and bit him. I desperately wanted a transfer.

A second reason was that I was sick of the cockroaches in the kitchen. At 4:30 a.m., after we'd turn on the kitchen lights, we'd see so many of these creepy things scampering around that it was scary. I was tired of having to squish them with my heavy steel-toed boots.

The third reason for desiring a transfer was the single most nauseating. The head baker, Candy, told me that she doesn't always wear gloves while baking because it's easier without them. That would not be such a big deal except for the fact that she had about five open wounds, cuts, and scrapes on her hands. The flour and sugar mixture was almost certainly coming into contact with her sores. I nearly threw up when I thought of it. I vowed never again to eat another dessert made in that kitchen.

Unfortunately, Mr. Tyler, a short compact man of about forty-five, refused to approve my request to transfer to the recreation department on the grounds that it might be looked upon as preferential treatment. Under prison regulations, you have to spend ninety days working in one job before you can switch jobs. Sometimes though, there are exceptions to the rule and you might be able to get a transfer. I prayed that God would work it out and get me out of the kitchen soon.

One bright spot in my work in the prison was teaching my essay class. It was good for me and kept my thoughts away from the disgusting kitchen duty. I felt joy when I gave of myself, knowing that I had something to share. I wasn't just building the ladies' self-esteem, but my own as well.

I'd get discouraged, now and then, though, because some of the women in my class wouldn't show up. At first, I thought they weren't happy to see me and didn't appreciate the fact I was there for them. Then I realized it wasn't about me. It was about them. It was about the loss of control, choice, and self they felt in prison. By deciding what they would attend and what they wouldn't, they were trying to keep alive the sense they had some control in their lives.

One inmate, Maria, came up to me one day and said, "Don't worry about it. We are grateful you come. Some of us don't get visits, and this is the only thing we look forward to."

Another guard who made our lives difficult was a thick-set, bearded man named Mr. Velasco who was put in charge of the commissary. He was one of the slowest supervisors ever. He took forever to scan and ring up our purchases. All of us women were convinced that if he had a job as a store cashier, he'd be promptly fired for poor performance.

As Mr. Velasco drove up, women were dashing from their rooms to the commissary as they normally do to get a good place in line.

"If I see anyone running over here anymore, I will send you to the back of the line," he shouted.

The women stopped in their tracks and huddled together.

"And if any of you fall down, bust your head, or hurt yourself, I won't even call medical for help."

That comment made my heart recoil. Carswell assures its inmates that they have access to medical care while there. I was very troubled by the cruelty and incongruity of the guard's statement.

During my incarceration, I discovered more and more about the frightening lack of even the most basic medical care. This alarming complacency and neglect added an extra layer of punishment over and above the prison sentences many of these women faced. So when

I felt sick to my stomach one day, I was scared and anxious because I had to go to my first "sick call" at the prison clinic. Sick call is held every morning, except for Wednesdays, Saturdays, and Sundays, from 6:45 a.m. to 7:45 a.m. If you don't arrive during that time, you have to wait until the next appointed day. And if you fall seriously ill, you have to report to the prison hospital, located across the street from where I was incarcerated.

"Do whatever you can to avoid going to that hospital," Victoria told me. "You'd be better off if they just buried you in the back of the prison, rather than go there."

I knew a little bit about what she was talking about. I had heard and read stories. An older inmate, Delinda, told me her horror story. "When I got to Carswell, my teeth were so rotten, that the dentist had to pull out every last one," she said.

"That wasn't the worse part. The dentist couldn't fit me with dentures for eighteen months! I lost nearly sixty pounds because I couldn't eat anything."

In the past, Carswell's hospital had a horrific trend of medical tragedies. Inmates often had to wait months to be assessed, let alone treated. I remember reading about a woman who discovered she had a lump in her breast and was pretty much ignored until the cancer spread to her back and spine. By the time she was admitted to the Carswell hospital and saw an oncologist, three months had passed, and she learned she had three months to live.

I got to the clinic promptly at 6:45 a.m. to make sure that my name got on the top of the list. But no one was there to let us in. I had to wait outside for an hour and fifteen minutes before the nurse and physician's assistant showed up. Also waiting were several other women, and most were much sicker than I was. I felt sorry for them because it was freezing cold outside. My fingers stiffened like icicles.

We were finally allowed to enter. Unsteadily, I wrote my name on the sign-in sheet. I was the fifth person on the list.

While waiting, I noticed Lily, an older Hispanic woman who was always very friendly to me. She was crying. It's one thing to see younger women crying but quite unsettling to see someone your mother or grandmother's age in tears. Another inmate consoled her, and they both were speaking in Spanish. But then her friend had to leave for work and Lily was left by herself. Her wide face looked tired and intensely worried. Her eyes were red and swollen.

"Do you need a hug?" I asked.

She said "yes" in a shaky whisper. So we hugged for a little while.

Lily explained to me that her uterus was dropping, and this had caused her an enormous amount of pain. Carswell hospital doctors diagnosed the condition several weeks ago but told her that if she refrained from doing anything strenuous, she'd be fine.

But Lily didn't get any better. She was getting worse, and the doctors were talking about surgery. Apparently, surgery can correct a pelvic disorder like hers. Lily was petrified, however. She had never had surgery before. But she was even more scared about having the procedure performed across the street.

The physician's assistant in the clinic said he couldn't do anything for her now, except prescribe some ibuprofen. He advised her to stay "idle" for a month. In prison lingo, "idle" meant to stay in your room except for meals and sick calls.

I never learned the outcome of Lily's situation. The medical complaints of women inmates were regularly ignored, according to my roommates. The presumption was that if you sought medical care, you weren't telling the truth or you wanted to get drugs. Inmates were pretty much discounted when it came to medical care in the prison system. The quality of medical care seemed dire, often resulting in actual harm due to failure to diagnose, refer, and treat.

My own visit with the physician's assistant, Mr. Snyder, was dismaying. He was like a robot just going through the motions. He barely heard what I had to say and made no eye contact. He gave me one week "idle." I realize prison isn't supposed to be a cushy place or the locale of luxury medical care, but any state that undertakes to incarcerate offenders must also undertake to meet certain basic needs for those offenders—one of which is safe, competent medical care. I was seriously rattled when I left the clinic. I entered hoping I'd be treated civilly and fairly; I left feeling very differently.

Another dismaying experience occurred the day a new guard by the name of Mrs. Payne came on duty—and she was a pain. A short, stocky woman with thick, black glasses, she called me into her office and snatched my ID from me.

"Are you wearing any underwear?" she yapped.

I was shocked by this, but I answered truthfully. "Yes, I'm wearing panties, but no bra."

I rarely wore a bra in prison, except while working out. It's just not something I think is necessary for me.

"Go back to your room and put a bra on immediately!" she demanded. "Or you'll get a shot."

A "shot" is an incident report, in which you're written up for disobedience.

I begrudgingly returned to my room to put on this unnecessary piece of clothing. I wondered whether it was a prison rule that we had to wear bras. I searched the forty-one–page rulebook, but I could find no such rule.

The next day, during mail call, the guard on duty—Mrs. Kroll— was horrible. As she read off our names, she kept mispronouncing them. Some of the inmates tried to correct her.

Mrs. Kroll got offended and yelled, "You guys need to shut the f—up!"

Later, my roommates told me that a few years ago, Mrs. Kroll was beaten up pretty badly by some of the inmates. Since then, she had been nasty and disrespectful to prisoners. That explanation put her attitude into better perspective for me.

Other guards simply found it entertaining to scare us—pounding unnecessarily loud on doors, shining lights directly in our faces, or making strip searches as humiliating and degrading as possible. Guards yielded tremendous power over us because we were in a controlled environment. I could understand their behavior if we were being combative, out of line, or violent, but we weren't. Guards seemed to get some kind of high just flexing their muscles and showing contempt.

Their behavior seemed almost Pavlovian to me. As a prisoner, I could see the current parallel our prisons bear to Pavlov's classical experiment. Inmates were like Pavlovian dogs, expected to respond to the jangling of keys by the guards. They wanted us to respond to them (or even to the sound of them) and ask for food or some other matter. They wanted us to jump at their every move. What better way to make these women feel less than human or submissive? After I realized this, I refused to respond or run to the door (like others did) when I heard those darn keys. Sure, I couldn't totally control my mind from responding, but I surely could control what my body does, and it wouldn't be standing at the door of cell 3109, salivating like a dog.

In the evenings, when many of the guards got off work, I would watch them as they walked to their cars. They looked so relieved that their day was over and that they were finally going home. I would think to myself: Do they ever think about the inmates? Do they ever give consideration to our life histories, family backgrounds, economic status, education, or chemical dependencies? Do they care? Or do they become so distant from it all that they don't even think about it anymore?

After observing the behavior of some of the guards toward inmates for a while, I thought to myself that something else had to be going on in their world. They must be dealing with a heavy burden that is, in and of itself, a self-made prison. Maybe that prison was a debt prison made of ruined credit, a marriage prison of shattered trust, a substance abuse prison with a ferocious addiction, or a low self-esteem prison of self-hate.

This got me thinking about the prisons many of us make for ourselves. As long as we're stuck in them, we can't do the things we need to do. *How could we break free?* I wondered.

Perhaps the answer lies in one of my favorite Bible stories: the story of Joseph in Genesis. It all began when Joseph was thrown into a pit and left to die by his jealous brothers. When some travelers came by, his brothers pulled him out and sold him to them. When the traveling merchants arrived in Egypt, they in turn sold him to an Egyptian official who eventually entrusted Joseph with overseeing his property. Joseph quickly rose to the top position in his master's home. But when the master's wife falsely accused the handsome, young Joseph of seducing her, he was put into prison. After some time, Joseph was released and appointed second-in-command over all of Egypt.

Joseph was faced with a whole run of circumstances that threatened to affect him adversely and that were beyond his control. His willingness to turn to God for the solution enabled him to make each experience a step of progress. He stayed close to God, no matter what his circumstances. And through it all, the Bible explains, "The Lord was with him, and that which he did, the Lord made it to prosper" (Genesis 39:23 KJV).

God had something far better planned for Joseph than he could imagine. And it seems to me that there's a promise in this for us all. God desires for us solutions and resolution, and He empowers us to find them. There is always an answer.

Many times we are faced with what feels like our own personal prison while we are waiting for a financial solution, a relationship resolution, or a healing to take place. The going will get tough and the hills will be hard to climb. It's important that during these times, we don't do anything foolish. I had to keep looking beyond my present circumstances and imagine the positive possibilities for my life. I had to overcome my emotions of feeling angry and overlooked and remind myself that "God has a plan for me."

The day will come when you will realize God hasn't forgotten you, that He wants you to be useful and purposeful and will empower you with endless opportunities so that you can be released from your own personal prison. No matter how messy your life gets, no matter how crazy your circumstances are, and no matter how much your heart is filled with fear and distress, God will rescue you.

The more I thought about those prison officials, I decided that they aren't bad people. They are only people who, in certain circumstances and conditions, do bad things. I prayed for them and my heart softened.

Most of the men and women who work in prisons, however, are

decent professionals who have never physically abused or intentionally degraded an inmate. There were plenty of guards who tried to do their jobs conscientiously under the trying conditions of a prison.

One example was Mr. Bell, a kindhearted guard who resembled a black Jiminy Cricket. There were many days when his job was demanding. For the growing number of women sent to prison, being incarcerated is not just about eating bad food and living in a tiny locked room. It is also about being submerged in a sexual subculture that exists only behind bars. It is widely known that there are a good number of gay women in female prisons. Though sexual relationships are prohibited, many female inmates have consensual sex in secretive places.

Guards sometimes catch them in the act. One time, an inmate alerted Mr. Bell that two women were secretly getting married. Mr. Bell rushed over there and quickly broke it up. The two women were sent to the SHU or the Security Housing Unit, as it is officially called. The SHU is a type of solitary confinement. Mr. Bell was just doing his job.

The prison environment can be very erotically charged. There were inmates who liked to flirt with some of the male prison guards. These women would put on their makeup, do their hair, and invent all kinds of reasons to see a particular guard or work double shifts just because the "guard of preference" was on duty. They thought nothing of sticking their assets out or putting an extra swing in their hips around certain male guards.

One day, in the kitchen, a fryer went out, and the chief maintenance person—a kind, respectful guy named Ruben with slicked down black hair—was called in to repair it. Within ten minutes, there were twenty-five women in the kitchen flirting with him and telling him how hot he was. Ruben just smiled, showing a gold tooth right off center, and winked at them.

Other guards are simply nice and treat you like a human being rather than a piece of trash. Once during a head count, one of the guards—Mr. Northrup—came in, pretending to dribble a basketball, and said, "Hey, MJ."

I was surprised, but thankful. Guards don't speak to us during counts, and we in turn have to keep quiet. I finally broke the silence by asking if he would be watching the Carolina game that night. I'm not sure why it made me feel so good that he acknowledged me personally. Maybe in my mind, I interpreted his behavior to mean that he supported me, even though I was locked up as an inmate.

Mr. Andrews, another guard, was very well liked by the inmates. He was an older man, but his steps were so lively that he could have been dancing. Mr. Andrews allowed families a little more "touchy-feely" time during their visits. One time, an inmate was sitting in the visitation room, crying her eyes out. Mr. Andrews walked over to her husband and said, "What are you waiting on? You better give her a hug or something."

While at Carswell, I searched my soul more and more. It struck me that I had a beautiful life and had taken it for granted. I was blessed with such a wonderful husband and children—this hit me like a flash. I thought a lot about my decision to do what was right and tell the truth, although the consequences had been great. When the chaplain for the prison's Saturday night church services spoke one evening about 1 Peter 2:19, I felt peace once again about my decision. The verse says: "For God is pleased with you when you do what you know is right and patiently endure unfair treatment" (NLT).

While I couldn't choose the things that happened *to* me, I did have the power to choose what happens *in* me. And so it was with my prison experience. I could let the troubles defeat and destroy me or let them stimulate a rate and depth of personal growth that isn't possible in calmer times. Every significant crisis in life is a turning point. Would I choose to allow the situation to corrupt my spirit and rob me of my future? No, I would choose the attitudes and behaviors that would enable me to recover emotional health, rediscover meaning in my life, and reformulate a plan for my future.

There were more hard-but-valuable tests to come, however. One night, an explosion of thunder rattled the windows of my room. I glanced out at the mass of dark clouds and shuddered. Spring in Texas meant thunderstorms, and this one looked bad. Lightning flashed in the window, quickly followed by another crash of thunder. Rain and wind pounded against the building, and golf ball–sized hail pelted the cars in the parking lot. I could hear the sound of a siren in the distance—a tornado warning. Other than being ordered to stay in our rooms, no other instructions were given for our safety. My mind was racing with thoughts about what I would do if a tornado did hit.

Fortunately, it didn't. But I wondered if this was a sign. Was another storm of life about to hit me?

CHAPTER 9

LOCKDOWN: ALONE FOR FORTY-EIGHT DAYS

She kept lunging at me. I fell down, hard, on the floor.

This woman was going to render me unconscious or she was going to kill me. There was no one to help me. She wouldn't stop, and after a while, I felt like my life was in danger. And I just lost it. I hit her in the face with my cooler and kicked her in the ribs.

The battle continued. She started fighting again and grabbed my hair. I tried to escape but she barred my exit from the room. With as much strength as I could gather, I vaulted toward the door, pushed it open, and ran down the corridor to the guard's station. She charged after me.

By now, there was plenty of evidence to show how vicious this five-minute fight had become. Her face was bruised and bloody. I, on the other hand, had no injuries. I had blocked her blows by shielding my face with my hands.

My assailant was Penny, thirty-four, one of my roommates. She got enraged after I asked that she not do my laundry anymore. I didn't explain why to her. It was just that too many of my things, too often, had turned up missing. Penny was from Plano, Texas, an affluent suburb of Dallas. To explain her prison sentence, she told the youngest of her five kids that she was going to a fat farm to lose weight.

The first time I met her, she seemed quiet. But the more I was around her, I could see that she was really standoffish, especially with me. Actually, she out-and-out hated me. She persisted in slamming the door whenever I was in the room. Around other inmates, she'd close it quietly. Once, when I came home from work for a good nap, she decided to ruin it by doing some room cleaning—something she could've easily postponed until I was finished napping.

I realize that people in close quarters with each other can easily become paranoid about each other and full of rage. But Penny, she was bad news.

We would both be able to explain our version of events, separately, at an evidentiary hearing to be held later. Until then, the fight earned us time in "the hole," prison lingo for being locked up in a cell twenty-three hours a day.

At Carswell, the hole is technically termed a "special housing unit," or SHU. I don't care what it's called; nothing comes close to describing the harrowing nature of this prison-within-a-prison. If someone were to ask me to identify the worst moment of my confinement, this was it. The SHU was like the next stop to hell.

Imagine spending all day every day trapped in a closet-sized, cement-walled cell, containing only a toilet in view of the guards, a sink, an iron bunk bed with a thin cushion, and a small, filthy shower with a transparent curtain and cold water (I wore socks while showering for fear of infection). There was no way to escape a cellmate's odors: the smell of sweat, breath, urine, and feces.

Prior to entering the SHU, I had to undergo a strip search, that degrading experience of being stripped naked in front of strangers who then examine every crevice and orifice of your body.

Shortly after being thrown in the SHU, I was handcuffed and brought to the Disciplinary Hearing Officer (DHO) room. A DHO is a certified disciplinary hearing staff member who can impose disciplinary sanctions on an inmate. The DHO was Lieutenant Stanley, a tall thin guard who walked with a slight stoop. He asked me to tell him, once again, what had happened during the altercation with Penny. I complied.

The only other people in the room were a secretary who transcribed what was being said and my chosen representative, Mr. Burke. In DHO hearings, all inmates are allowed to choose one representative to ensure that their rights are not violated. This is another joke, because if you really want to get technical about it, it's not like your rep is non-partial. Representatives are paid by the BOP (Bureau of Prisons), not by any third party company or organization. Nonetheless, I selected Mr. Burke because he seemed like a kind and fair guy.

A man by the name of Mr. Muncy materialized on a wide-screen TV via webcast in the room, reigning ominously like Big Brother over the proceedings. He recited my name, number, and rights. He then asked me for my version of the incident.

Next, he informed me that three witnesses were going to testify on my behalf. Those witnesses corroborated my story, mainly that they saw me fleeing from the room first, with Penny chasing after me. In the end, of course, nothing the witnesses said or anything I said mattered. Mr. Muncy found me guilty of fighting and disregarded my self-defense claim.

He sanctioned me to be held in the SHU for thirty days. In all, it would stretch out to forty-eight days. He also took away my email, commissary, and visitation privileges for ninety days. The last one, visitation, hurt me the most because it meant I wouldn't be able to see Oba, or anyone else for that matter, for three months. I could really care less about the commissary or email, but it really made life that much tougher not to be able to talk to Oba face to face.

I was granted only one fifteen-minute phone call a month. This made me feel a million miles away from Monty and Amir. Not getting a chance to hear their voices was the worst punishment of all of this, enough to drive me mad.

I decided to appeal the sanctions, which was within my rights. I learned that I probably wouldn't hear anything back from the DHO before ninety days. A lot of good filing an appeal would do. I concluded that the appeal process was intended for those who had longer sentences than mine. Nonetheless, I went through the necessary hoops for the sake of it. But nothing ever came of my appeal.

In the SHU, I was alone. I was at the mercy of merciless guards. I was cut off from the world. I was vulnerable. I was depressed. All I wanted to do was to get out.

My room had a white toilet and sink right out in the open, with no real privacy. I was surrounded by other rooms occupied by other inmates. It created an environment unlike any other. The noise was deafening at times. Women would yell back and forth to and over each other. Often, they'd bang on the door to get the attention of the guard for reasons ranging from a medical complaint to a disgruntled and frustrated individual who was banging just to be banging. Everyday, I would hear the doors clank shut behind me, and I'd be reminded once again that I was a prisoner.

My sight of the outside world was through a small, slot-like window. At night I'd look for the changing faces of the moon and whatever stars might come into my view. It gave me a renewed appreciation for the beauty of our world. I would never again take a window for granted.

I was issued an oversized canvas jumpsuit—a bright orange one so that everyone knows you are in the SHU. I was allowed to receive and send mail as normal. But since all letters incoming and outgoing are read, letters are routinely rejected.

Letters to me from my children, thankfully, were not discarded. Monty sent me a picture he drew himself. It was a drawing of me with a diamond tooth, diamond shoes, and a diamond shirt. Most touching was that he signed it, "We love you, Mommy." I broke down and bawled.

I was barred from teaching my essay class, and this troubled me. I had already let so many people down; now I felt like I had let women at Carswell down at an important juncture in their lives—and with an important need that would now be unfulfilled. I didn't know if I could make it up to them. The mantra of "finish what you start, do it well, and don't be a quitter" had been drilled into me from a young age. Now I couldn't live up to that promise.

Time in the SHU would grind to a near halt. I kept three or four books going at the same time so I didn't get bored. I saw it as switching channels on television. You know, when you get tired and fed up with one, you go on to the next. The four white walls and the lack of any real human interaction started to weigh heavily on me.

The passage of minutes was marked by the constant, annoying jingle of keys on a guard's waistband, the screams of other inmates, and the scraping of a food tray through the slot in the door by a pair of disembodied hands. I had to be handcuffed to leave the cell and strip-searched to return, accompanied at all times by at least one armed guard.

Pat-downs after leaving the cell and before returning to it were almost always done by a man. Fortunately, I was never brushed, touched, or patted down on the breast, buttocks, or private areas by the male officers. Pat-downs were a joke, in my opinion. Guards patted areas in which it was almost impossible to conceal anything—legs, arms, and back. They also made you take off your clunky shoes so they could look at the bottoms of your feet.

Whenever I was escorted to the visitation room, the guard with me forced all the inmates we passed in the hallway to turn and face the wall. I didn't know if this was special treatment for me or if it was customary for everyone coming from the SHU. A few women recognized me and hollered my name. Their acknowledgments brought a smile to my face.

During any visitation, I had to sit in the first row of seats right in front of the guards. I wasn't permitted to move around except to go to the bathroom.

I wasn't allowed to purchase any snacks or drinks. Only the most basic items were offered to me, such as toiletry items, batteries, stamps, and stationary. The toothbrush they issued to me was as tiny as Monty's pinky finger.

Sundays were my hair washing days. I'd put some hot oil moisturizer on my hair and wrap it with the two pieces of plastic wrap that covered the food trays. It made a good, deep conditioning for my hair, however comical looking.

The food was horribly substandard. One meal consisted of leathery meat patties and something that was swimming around in an inedible cream sauce. Everything was mostly served cold. I knew I wouldn't be getting proper nutrition while in the SHU. I asked one of the lieutenants if I could purchase a bottle of vitamin supplements from the commissary, even though my commissary privileges had been suspended. He agreed and one of the guards brought me some vitamins, plus a bottle of vitamin C that I had in my personal property. I was so thankful. These experiences taught me to be thankful for the little things—a form of thankfulness that prepares our hearts for the bigger things that come into our lives.

One hour a day, I was taken outside to the recreation yard for exercise. But I was placed in a cage.

There were five or six cages all around the yard for other inmates. One lady, confined to a wheelchair, was in a cage. I heard her arguing with the guard about how ridiculous it was for her to be in handcuffs, too, since she couldn't move out of the wheelchair. Other women were heavily medicated and just sat in their cages, staring vacantly into the sky. I wondered how they got like that. What event or events took place in their lives that could cause their brains to go astray at such early ages? And then I began to immediately thank God for blessing me with my wits. I felt compassion for these women who looked eternally lonely and asked God to bless them with strength and favor.

Another time, while exercising in my cage, I overhead one inmate tell another that she was in the SHU for pouring boiling water on her girlfriend's back and burning her. She expressed no remorse and even said she wished she had burned her face. Apparently, this was a lover's quarrel.

Since I had only had one hour in my cage, I planned out my time very efficiently in order to get as productive a workout as I could. I'd do jumping jacks in my socks, as well as hops and lunges. After a few minutes, I had to roll up my orange jumpsuit pants because the sweat was starting to pour off me. It was nearly ninety degrees at only six in the morning.

The sweltering heat and activity made me parched and thirsty. I needed water. You'd think that a simple request such as a glass of water wouldn't be too much to ask for, but apparently it was. My request was denied. I wondered if someone collapsed because of heat exhaustion or dehydration, would the prison change its policy? I had to do the unthinkable: drink some water from the disgusting faucet in my cell.

While in my room one evening, I overheard the guards talking about some of the women in the psych ward at Carswell. The guards were speaking of incidents in which inmates would eat their own feces or smear it on the windows or women who were "cutters" and would self-mutilate their bodies. I was very disappointed at how they were telling the stories, almost jokingly and so callously. I lay down on my bunk and put on my headphones to drown out the guards' voices.

Every two weeks, the guards moved prisoners to different rooms, usually to the one right next door. I guess this was to prevent anyone from having enough time to dig an escape hole, like you see in prison flicks. I wondered what the prison thought we'd dig with: a pencil or that tiny toothbrush they supplied?

The second room to which I was assigned was filthy, full of dust and black stuff on the walls. Whoever resided there before me apparently never cleaned anything. I spent two hours scrubbing the beds, floors, walls, shower, sink, and toilet. I organized my books, letters, and toiletry items. I was happy because I had something to occupy my brain and body for a few hours, without having to peek at the clock radio to watch time creep by.

Around mid-April, I received a letter from a cousin on my father's side. He sent a few pictures of the Jones family. It is weird to see people who resemble you but whom you don't know. Reading his letter brought back some painful memories of my father's funeral. In 2002, he had been found dead in the bathroom of his home. He must have had a heart attack or a stroke and fallen and knocked his head. Thankfully, a girlfriend of my father's knew that he had this famous daughter and found me on the Internet and called my management company to let me know the news of his passing. I sat down. I had no idea what to think or feel. It was completely out of the blue. My emotions were a mess, a mixture of sadness and resentment. He had always ignored my letters, my birthdays, me. I traveled to California to clear up his estate and attend his funeral.

It was weird. There was a picture of a young George Jones next to his open coffin. I sat in the front row with the family—and watched one person after another eulogize my father. The pastor asked me if I wanted to say anything, but I declined. What did I have to say? Nothing positive, nothing really at all. I didn't know the man. Even so, I was crying. I was crying because I didn't know him.

Among the speakers were several young people about my age who got up with tears streaming down their faces and said he was like a father to them. It broke my heart to hear this. How could he have been so wonderful to these girls and so horrible and distant to me? How can he save the best of himself for these girls and show his only daughter a monster? That was the hardest part. I felt like getting up at the end and revealing the truth about this man named George Washington Jones that everyone would miss—even adored.

Life gives us very terrible, sometimes inescapable, trials that we have to go through, and I was going through another one. I started thinking negative thoughts. I thought about the fact that when I did get out, I wouldn't have one dime to put Monty into school, let alone money to buy his school supplies. I didn't have a dime to go to Sam's Club to buy dinner for our family. I didn't have one dime to pay my monthly cell phone bill. I felt like such a failure and disappointment.

One afternoon, I bolted upright in my bunk and told myself to snap out of it. I made the decision to shake off the negativity. It all went back to my sports days. When I played basketball at the University of North Carolina, I'd think about how difficult it was to win away from home, and that negative thought would drip into my subconscious and trip me up. I had to squeeze out all negative thoughts and replace them with positive thoughts like, "I love playing away from home and I enjoy the challenge." Positive statements like that helped me perform better every time. That's how I learned the power of positive thinking. It works for anyone who wants to lead a successful life.

While in the SHU, I'd shift my thinking from the dread of not seeing Oba for three months to the highly anticipated moment when, in twenty-five days, I'd get to hear Monty, Amir, and Oba's voices on the phone.

Being in the SHU also got me thinking about Nelson Mandela, who endured twenty-seven years in prison, including a decade of solitary confinement. A favorite memory of mine is meeting Nelson Mandela in South Africa. Someone from the government office called my hotel room wondering if I'd like to meet him. I was over the moon. Nelson Mandela! Nelson Mandela had asked to meet me! Would I like to meet him? What kind of question was that? Of course, I'd like to meet him!

I had been driven up to the Mandela estate, and there was the great man himself, waiting to greet me. Immediately I was struck by the aura around him. He is a magnetic presence. He radiates positive energy and makes everyone in the room feel wonderful. I found him playful, almost childlike, in the obvious joy he has for life. I had no idea what I said to him; I was so awestruck. I'm sure I mumbled something coherent. He told me, "I'm a big fan, and I wish you the best of luck." It was altogether one of the best experiences of my life.

Those of us who watched Nelson Mandela in 1990 as he walked into the light of freedom were stunned that we did not see a bitter man hobbling, shakily hanging onto a cane. Instead we saw a man walking straight with an energy that belied his seventy-three years. *How*, I wondered, *did he do it? How did he manage?* We were told it was his faith in God, his spiritual strength.

Whenever I felt negative, I prayed or reached for my Bible. One of my favorite, most sustaining pieces of Scripture while I was in the SHU was this: "Therefore do not be anxious about tomorrow, for tomorrow will be anxious for itself. Sufficient for the day is its own trouble" (Matthew 6:34 ESV). That passage always put me at so much peace about my future and the future of my family and blessed me with hope.

In the SHU, you feel like you're placed on hold—like "The Waiting Place" in the Dr. Seuss book *Oh, the Places You Go* that I read to my kids. It's that "weirdish wild space . . . a most useless place . . . for people just waiting." I kept recalling more words in that great book: "NO! That's not for you! Somehow you'll escape all that waiting and staying. You'll find the bright places where Boom Bands are playing."

Oh, God, bring on the Boom Bands, please!

It was easy to feel discouraged. It was easy to wonder if God had forgotten me in that waiting place.

Though I prayed and asked God for help, it often seemed that God was slow in responding. What do you do when you're waiting on God?

I kept on doing what I knew was right. I read my Bible. I prayed.

I stayed positive. I kept my faith. I hung on to his promises. I clung to hope.

One of my favorite foods is ice cream. When I think of eating it, my taste buds are activated. And even though I'm not eating it, my taste buds are pleasurably anticipating something that will soon be experienced. That's what hope is to me. It causes me to anticipate joyfully my future. It overcomes my anxiety and dread. I might be in a problem-filled present, but hope tells me that better things are coming my way. In more words from Dr. Suess: "There is fun to be done! There are points to be scored. There are games to be won."

My faith evoked miracles. One day, I was informed by a guard that an anonymous woman from a Fort Worth church sent a blessing my way in the form of $210 added to my commissary account. I asked the guard if she had any other information as to what church, and she responded by saying that the lady only wanted me to know that there were people out there who were praying and supporting me. I took a deep breath and thanked God. I was overwhelmed by a rush of pure gratitude so powerful that I couldn't even speak.

With this woman's loving gesture, one of Jesus's parables took concrete form: "I was hungry and you gave me something to eat, I was thirsty and you gave me something to drink, I was a stranger and you invited me in, I needed clothes and you clothed me, I was sick and you looked after me, I was in prison and you came to visit me" (Matthew 25:35–36 NIV).

Faith is an amazing thing. Hebrews 13:6—a book of the Bible that encourages us to hold on to our profession of faith in God—tells us: "The Lord is my helper, I will not fear: What can man do to me?" (NKJV).

I have answered that question like this: They can lock me up. They can lock up my body. They can take away all my freedoms. But what's inside of me—what's inside my heart, mind, and spirit—is mine. They can't take that. They can't lock that up.

I knew God had His hand on me. But you won't believe what happened next.

CHAPTER 10

SHACKLED: WHEN YOU FEEL LIKE A FAILURE

The memory of what happened to me next is so vivid that I will tell it as if it is happening only today.

There is a loud, obnoxious bang on the door of my lockdown cell at three in the morning.

"Pack your bag. You're getting on a bus."

I have thirty minutes to get ready, barely enough time to pack what little I am allowed to bring. I quickly wash my hair, wrap it in bun with three hair ties, and dash off a very short letter to my husband and Rich Nichols that I am leaving Carswell.

My destination is San Francisco to testify in the trial of my former coach, who is being prosecuted for making false statements to a federal agent in connection with the BALCO investigation.

A couple of weeks earlier, I had been tipped off by one of the guards that I'd be leaving the prison temporarily on a "Writ." A Writ is a written order, issued by a court, ordering someone to do (or stop doing) something. While exercising in my cage one day, this

125

guard said to me, out of the blue: "You know, you're headed out west, right?"

I didn't want to look surprised because then he might have thought that he shouldn't have told me and not give me any more information. As I continued to walk, I told him that I had heard it was a possibility and was not surprised.

The day has come. Silently, the guards herd me down cement floor corridors and into the processing area where I am able to shed my horrid-looking orange jumpsuit for some khakis. I am patted down by a jowl-faced female guard, who, if not quite middle-aged, has a thickening above her waist that makes her quite matronly. The alcohol on her breath broadcasts in my direction. During the normal but humiliating strip search, I sort of leave my body and retreat into my mind, thinking only of my family and the day I will be reunited with them. The knot in my stomach loosens considerably after that.

The guard is looking for contraband. She finds some in the form of my hair ties. She cites them as an infraction and takes them away from me. My hair falls in unruly clumps. I decide to braid what I can and tuck the rest into the hair at the nape of my neck.

Next, I am handcuffed and shackled at the ankles in three-pound leg irons and escorted to an awaiting bus. Unsteady, I limp and stumble as I walk. The shackles are so tight that I feel like my ankles are bleeding. I ask the guard if she can loosen them.

"Oh, you'll be all right, Jones."

In addition to this woman, there is another guard accompanying us on the ride. He is a strapping, round-faced chain smoker with a small black mustache. He has taken a special dislike to me for once reporting that he was smoking on the premises. I strongly disapprove of smoking, especially in prison where secondhand smoke is a real danger. As we file onto the bus, he stands next to the longest rifle I have ever seen.

I hear the door slam shut. The bus wheezes and starts to roll forward.

"You do not speak! You do not sing!" He screams so loudly that no one will dare oppose him.

It is freezing on the bus. My fingernails turn blue. My teeth chatter. My hands shake. I bury my head in my shirt. The only warmth I feel are the tears rolling down my cheeks.

There is a bathroom in the back of the bus. I need to use it, so I falter clumsily to the back. The toilet is tiny, no doors, just a pot to pee in, as my mother used to say. Nobody pays any attention to me, so I decide to urinate. But I can't pull my pants and underwear down. How will I wipe, with handcuffs, shackles, and a heavy chain around my waist?

I finally give up. I resign myself to the idea that men probably don't wipe or shake, anyway, and just stick it back in their pants. After about five minutes in the back, I emerge. Four ladies are waiting in line. I apologize and return to my bus seat.

We pull into a truck stop and park there for about thirty minutes.

The sky turns black. Rain falls in vast sweeps. The moan of the wind is deafening. The guards look worried.

"Put your heads in your lap!" the male guard shouts. "Keep your bodies away from the window. Stick your legs in the aisle!"

We look at him like he is crazy, because there is no way, with chains, shackles, and handcuffs on, that we can pull off this maneuver. He realizes his mistake. He instructs us to put our heads on our laps and pray for the best.

The only person I know on the bus is Brenda, a forty-seven-year-old Jewish woman from Alabama. She is short and round with teased brown hair. She had been confined to the SHU for several months for failing numerous drug tests. Her drug of choice is oxycontin, which she tells me is easily obtainable in the prison.

Brenda has been in Carswell for ten years and has another fifteen to go for refusing to rat on a drug dealer. She will not get out of prison until her eleven-year-old daughter is twenty-six. Her family no longer visits her. I do not know her full story, but it tears at my heart. Her sentence seems so excessive. I once asked her how she is able to do it. She answered without hesitation: "Because I have no other choice."

Brenda is the person I give all my magazines to when I am finishing reading them. To thank me for the magazines, she made me a pen decorated with cool colors and tape. I don't know how she crafted it, but it is one of the nicest gifts anyone has ever made for me, especially because pens are impossible to come by in Carswell, and most letters had to be written using pencils. Brenda is being transferred to a women's prison in Danbury, Connecticut.

The bus travels on, away from the virulent storm. Eventually, it arrives at a prisoner transfer site in Oklahoma City.

We are temporarily deposited into a room with nothing but a long bench, a toilet, and sink. We are then able to speak freely to each other. I learn from the conversation that most of the inmates know who I am. It amuses me to see people's reactions after they meet me. One woman says she didn't realize I am so tall; another says she thought I might be stuck-up.

Because I am technically still a SHU prisoner, I am put into the prison's SHU for my stay there. I have a roommate here whose name is Saioa, age thirty-two. She is a petite Chinese woman with roughly cut black hair. Saioa speaks no English. She cannot converse with anybody and spends most of her time in the room working on a puzzle, one with missing pieces. She has to be told to do everything, from going to the pill line for medication to standing in the cafeteria line for meals. I decide to spend the evening with her, doing the puzzle. No more than ten words are spoken between us. But figuring out the puzzle bonds us with the universal language of accomplishment. After successfully completing it, we high-five each other.

The transfer center here is for both male and female inmates. The men and women like to talk to each other, although it is forbidden. An odd type of communication system has been developed between them, even though they can't see each other. They dip a cup into the toilet to empty it. Then they clean the toilet with disinfectant. Next, they connect empty toilet paper rolls and thread them down deep through the commodes. The connected rolls operate like makeshift megaphones. Speaking through the rolls, a woman can talk to a man on the floor above her.

I listen to the quality of the sound. It is amazingly clear. If someone wants to "make a call," they use their cups to talk inside the toilet. So, every night, after lockdown at 9:30 p.m., you hear these taps from all over the place. I am learning how resourceful prisoners can be. But I decide that this is a very unsanitary practice, and I wonder if it is responsible for the sores I see on the inmates' mouths.

After a few days, I am boarded on an unmarked jetliner with other prisoners. The plane is part of the Justice Prisoner and Alien Transportation System, otherwise known as "ConAir." It will fly more than two hundred thousand federal prisoners this year to prisons and courtrooms around the country. Its past passenger list has included televangelist Jim Bakker and would-be assassins Lynette "Squeaky" Fromm and John Hinckley.

At first blush, the plane looks like any other jet. But when you look closely, you see that the tray tables and other moveable parts have been taken out, because marshals fear the inmates might use them to fashion weapons. The tough-looking marshals who fly ConAir carry no firearms on board, only electronic stun guns. Like Air Force One, a ConAir jet has priority over other aircraft for takeoff.

On my flight, the prisoners, mostly men, are a brute bunch of vile thugs and sickos. Their arms are mottled with tattoos of swastikas and skulls and cross bones. One has the torso of someone who appears to have spent many hours lifting weights in the prison yard.

Pedophiles and sex offenders—the neighbors nobody wants—are seated up front. How to describe them? Two are old and grizzled. One has blondish-brown hair, about thirtyish with a barrel chest. The six or so of us women are seated behind them, and then the rest of the men are behind the women.

The bathroom is in the back of the plane. To get there, you have to snake past the tattoo crowd, who, I have been warned, will hiss at the women and try to brush up against them. My bladder is full and very uncomfortable. Nonetheless, I decide to hold it until we land.

Although I am chained to my seat, I feel disconnected to everything, a failure. I have failed as a daughter, a mother, a sister, friend, role model, and wife. It is one of my most awful, darkest moments.

Have you ever felt like that? The fact is each of us will, at one time or another. We will feel acutely that we have missed the mark, that we are a failure in achieving a goal, a disappointing conclusion, a downfall. That reality, however, must be balanced by this greater reality: failure is never final. It is not the finish line. It is a setback, yes—but it is a temporary event and ultimately, a situation which can be rectified, remedied, repaired, and risen above.

I can't say I have any special knowledge about how to tower over failure, only experience. I learned to protect my thoughts. I couldn't allow myself to be seduced by the idea that one failure meant I was a complete failure. If you are thinking along those lines, I would say, avoid compounding one failure into many by shaming and blaming yourself unduly. Don't let distractions like fear and doubt creep into your brain, because that's what ruins you.

We take off from Oklahoma City and fly to Pueblo, Colorado. Some inmates get off; some new ones get on.

The next leg of the trip is to Salt Lake City, Utah. More prisoners are transferred on and off. I am starving. The last morsel of food I ate was a mini chocolate muffin in Oklahoma City.

The plane takes off. We are served lunch: four peanut butter crackers, a granola bar, a bruised apple, poked with holes, and a small bottle of water. I devour everything, except the apple. I want to drink the water, but I am afraid it will overload my already painful bladder, so I opt against it.

The next stop is the desert city of Victorville, California. At the Victorville Federal Correctional Complex, everyone is ushered off the plane. Unless I get to a bathroom soon, I will wet my pants. As I pass a line of buses, I ask the sheriff if he will let me use the bathroom in one of the buses. He recognizes me and permits it.

The sheriff is a kind man. "The only time I'd beat you in a race is now, with those shackles on your feet," he quips. "I am a big fan, and I wish you the best." God is shining down on me.

We board a bus to take us to San Bernardino, my next destination. During the ride, we pass the exit for Palmdale. Palmdale is where I got my first exposure to organized sports. In my mind, I transport myself back to happier times.

I am seven years old. Ira is drilling a hole in our driveway for a tetherball pole and also a basketball goal. All the kids come over for contests. Mom and Ira and the other parents bring their chairs out on warm evenings and chat while we play basketball or soccer or ride our bikes. Later, I am in the front yard barefoot doing handstands, cartwheels, and flips—the entire routine I learned in gymnastics class. I turn around and see my beloved Ira, looking out the window at me, smiling and acting proud. I finish my routine with my hands stretched over my head like the gymnasts do at the end of their routine. He tells me how proud he is of me. I feel great. I feel happy. And I feel loved. When you hit low points, it helps to revisit past successes or times in your life when you felt or experienced joy. This makes you feel whole and worthy again.

We arrive at San Bernardino County prison, and I'm placed in the SHU overnight. I remember stories I had heard about the conditions at county jails, and they weren't good. Rumor had it they were filthy—the worst places to be housed—and the food is deplorable. The rumors are true.

The cell was about half the size of my closet at home. It had one bed, a toilet, a sink, and no windows. There is no way to flush the toilet, except to ask a guard to use a plunger. The smell of garbage and unwashed bodies is overpowering. I am allowed to rinse off in a shower that works only occasionally. It is slimy, and the chipped floor tile is filled with black mold. I rush in and out as quickly as possible.

I am at a low point again. I feel sorry for myself. I feel completely hollow. I spend most of my time reading, writing letters, and watching television. At night, I cry myself to sleep. I didn't sign up for this.

The next day, we are bused back to the Victorville airport, where the federal plane is waiting for us. For forty minutes, the guards force us to stand outside the plane in chilling thirty-five–degree weather with high winds. I can't put my hands in my shirt to warm them, because I am handcuffed. My only recourse is to think of warm places I have visited. Belize, Barbados. Las Vegas. Miami.

Finally, the plane takes off. After an hour, we land on a small airstrip at the Fairfield Airport in northern California. I am ordered to board a van where two U.S. marshals are waiting for me. We take a forty-minute drive to the Alameda County Jail, in Oakland, California.

Finally, my shackles and handcuffs are removed. I check to see if there is any blood on my ankles, but there is none, thankfully.

Two female guards put me in a room where I will be housed by myself. The room has a phone and television set. I am issued a red uniform. The guards give me their cards and tell me to let them know if I need anything. I feel like I have returned to some semblance of civilized living. The hardest part, though, is that my wedding ring is confiscated. Wearing jewelry is not allowed because other inmates will steal it. I immediately call my husband, and although I break down in tears, I feel better.

Most mornings, I stay in bed as long as I can because the more time I'm asleep, the less time that I have to live in this nightmare.

It is Amir's first birthday. It is bittersweet because I am unable to share it with him. I sing him "Happy Birthday" over the phone, but he is not very interested. He is distracted by whatever else is going on in the room. To ease my pain, I sit down and write him a special birthday poem.

My Sweet Baby Amir, on your first birthday!
I long to see your smile and hear your voice.
The one who captured my heart
Without me having a choice.
Distance separates us,
On this, your special day.
Our love is everlasting,
It can never be swayed.
You might not recognize me when we see each other again,
But I am confident
That our everlasting bond will win.
That when that glorious day comes
When we can reunite,
Our love will remind us
Of that first night.

When I looked in your eyes

And touched your sweet face,

And told you no matter the time or the place,

Mommy will be there

To guide you along your way.

And so, here we are, a year from that day.

Celebrating your life in an inconceivable way.

Mommy is far,

Unable to witness

The light in your eyes

From your first birthday wishes.

I want you to know, though,

That although I wasn't there,

I celebrated with you

The joy in the air.

My youngest son,

You turned one today,

Are getting so big.

God has answered my prayers.

My Sweet Amir,

Our little prince,

A life so precious,

We are convinced.

Happy First Birthday, Mir Mir.

We love you!

Mommy

I decide to focus on gratitude. With gratitude in my heart, there is no room for self-pity, resentment, or bitterness. Gratitude attracts more blessings, especially when we humbly and joyfully express our thanksgiving to God and to those who have encouraged us. From gratitude, I find excitement, joy, and greater appreciation for life.

Oba's parents are raising my sons right now, and for that, I am grateful. I thank God that they opened their hearts and took on the stress of caring for two boys under the age of five. Monty and Amir are safe and loved immensely. Who could ask for more than that?

I am also grateful for the little things, like the newspaper the guards bring me every day. I immerse myself in reading every single article and comic. I take my time completing the sudoku, crossword, and word jumble puzzles.

The guards check on me throughout the night, but they do not come inside my room, nor do they flash lights in my eyes or jangle their keys.

The conditions under which I have been living are soul crushing. Nonetheless, I must make myself speak in ways that empower me. Examples: rather than say, "It's a big problem," I'd say, "It's a big opportunity." Rather than say, "This is terrible," I'd say, "This is a learning experience." Rather than say, "It's hopeless," I'd say, "God will show me ways to open a new door."

More than anything right now, I want my life to turn around. My faith assures me that this will happen. Because I believe in the all-sufficiency and omnipotence of God, I know that Jesus always turns everything around. The Bible says so: The first shall be the last and the last shall be first; the prostitutes will enter the Kingdom of Heaven before the Pharisees.

No matter how messy our lives get, no matter how crazy our circumstances are, and no matter how much our hearts are filled with fear and distress, we can all be clear about one thing, and that is that there is nothing too hard for God. There are no problems that are too complex, no wounds that are too deep, no challenge too far gone for God to reverse.

I have been taken on the ConAir journey—all to no avail. I never did testify at that trial. I am informed that I am returning to Carswell.

CHAPTER 11

TEACHING MY CHILDREN TO DO WHAT'S RIGHT

One by one, the inmates trickled into the prison visiting room at Carswell. Their faces broke into joyful grins when they saw their waiting children. A little girl, with a blonde ponytail and a pink polka dot dress, skipped over to meet her mom. After a tight hug, the two walked hand in hand to a quiet corner so the mother could adjust her daughter's ponytail. The embraces of mother and daughter were genuine, the cries of "Mommy" heartrending.

These reunions were enough to illustrate the difference between inside and outside, freedom and the lack of it. It was humbling to see the sacrifice and love that people have for their family members, even though they messed up and brought shame and disgrace to the family. If not for the faithful husbands and grandmothers and grandfathers and other family members who take the kids, mostly toddlers, to see their mothers, all prisons would be much darker pits of despair.

I witnessed an emotional scene where a six-month-old baby was placed in his young mother's loving arms. She gave birth to him one week before she was incarcerated. I cried for that baby.

Then I cried for my babies. Once I was back at Carswell, the pain of being separated from Monty and Amir worsened, the loneliest part of everything. I longed to pick them up and twirl them around like the other mothers were doing. I began to question my decision to send them to their grandparents in Barbados for six months. I was worried that the bond I developed with Amir, who was only eight months old when I was sent to prison, might disappear into thin air. Will he know me? Will he want to come to me? That was really the hardest part. At least, with Monty, he's old enough to remember who Mommy is. But, with Amir, he's not, and with him, it will be like meeting a stranger. I tried not to think about it too much, but sometimes I couldn't help it. They're my babies, and my connection with them is endless. I was scared. I have heard that separation from a parent is a traumatic event that can have lifelong consequences. I prayed not.

As I touched on earlier, Monty's fifth birthday passed while I was in prison. My first child. Five years old. A huge milestone for both of us. The best I could do was have Oba make a short videotape of me talking to Monty about his birthday and the importance of turning five.

I stretched out on my bunk. Above me were pictures of Monty and Amir. I taped them there so that I would always see them the first thing in the morning and the last thing at night. It was tough not being able to tuck them up in bed at night or be there when they woke up crying.

Monty and Amir. I smiled every time I said their names. Both boys represent the parts of me that are good, happy, and carefree. I prayed for them every night: *God please put your arms over them and protect them.* I just wanted to get home and be with my husband and children.

I often thought about what I will tell my children about going to prison, about other things. They'd learn that I was a fast runner; they'd learn that I was in the Olympics. But how would I explain why I don't have any medals? How would I tell them that I was locked up for six months in 2008? How would I tell them to be careful of the decisions they make because they carry consequences, regardless of intent? What would I tell my children about lying when I had done it myself?

I decided that I would tell them the truth. I would tell my children that I once lost my path and made the wrong decisions. I wanted them to know that I am not perfect, but that I grew through my mistakes. I believe this can be a very important lesson about what it is to be human.

While the memories were still fresh and vivid, I wrote down on paper what I would tell my boys. Maybe someday I would read these words to them or just tell them directly:

"Monty and Amir, I want you to know that you both are the most beautiful gifts that any person could ever receive. God has blessed me in so many ways throughout my life, but having you as my children and Daddy as my husband are the ultimate blessings. Please understand and never doubt this, no matter who tries to tell you otherwise.

"In 2008, I went to a place in Texas called Carswell, while you stayed with your grandparents in Barbados and had many happy times.

"Mommy was in this place because I had to be here, not because I wanted to be. I was there because I made a mistake in life. Because of this mistake, I had to pay a horrible price, which temporarily separated me from you and Daddy.

"This place where Mommy lived for six months is called prison or jail. I was there because I lied, because I made a decision several years ago to hide the truth for fear that all of our lives would be changed. What Mommy didn't realize at that time was that this lie would forever impact all of our lives. It created lots of pain and caused all of our friends and family shame, disappointment, and heartache.

"Maybe right now, you are asking, 'Well, why, Mommy, did you do this to all of us, why?' And the answer is both simple and not so simple.

"Perhaps the most obvious, simple, and honest answer is because I wanted to protect everyone around me as well as myself. I wanted to preserve all of my hard work and dedication. I wanted to secure our futures. I wanted to protect you both from the harsh realities of the world.

"These are my simple and obvious reasons for telling this lie. They are straightforward and honest and I hope you can understand some-what why I made this decision. It was wrong in hindsight. If I had to do it over again, I would not do what I did and I would not lie.

"Babies, what it comes down to is this: Mommy made a terrible mistake, one that cost me something more valuable and priceless than money can buy. My mistake cost me Monty and Amir for six months of our lives. These are six months that I can never get back, ever.

"Never listen to or rely on what you read in newspapers or magazines or what you see on TV for the truth. If you ever want to talk about the truth about what happened to me, come and ask Mommy and Daddy, and we will tell you.

"I love you both more than the breath I take."

———————■———————

More than ever, I am committed to raising my children so that they are kind, honest, and loving, and so they don't make the same mistakes as I did. I am not an expert or professional in parenting. I'm just a mom and an imperfect one, at best.

I want to try to set the same example my mother set for me while I was growing up. My mom had codes of conduct in our home. We weren't allowed to curse, for instance; in our household, saying "hell" was bad enough—we didn't even know the f-word.

Mom was a wonderful teacher when it came to manners. Growing up, I was taught to say "thank you" and "please" for every occasion.

I was taught to always address adults with "ma'am" or "sir." I was so thoroughly indoctrinated in my ma'ams and sirs that on a television interview with Oprah Winfrey, I would answer her with my "Yes, ma'am." She was amused by my politeness and told me I didn't have to call her "ma'am."

Learning manners taught me more than about just being polite. It taught me the value of kindness, thoughtfulness, respect, and patience. If you have manners, you offer to help someone who is physically challenged or has an armful of groceries. If you have manners, you give up your seat to someone older, infirm, or pregnant. If you have manners, you don't shove or rush to the head of the line; you are patient and wait your turn. If you have manners, you hear someone out; you don't talk over them, raise your voice, or interrupt. You actually listen. My mom taught me these things, and I want to pass them down to my children.

As my mother did, Oba and I realize that we are our children's biggest moral influence. We have decided what fabric of morality will unfold in our families. Our priorities as a family, for example, are kindness, honesty, and the love of God. We are dedicated to living by them and passing these priorities along to our children. If I want to instill a certain value (say, honesty) in my children, I will be on the lookout every day for ways to illustrate my point.

One day I walked in on my three-year-old, Monty, who had crayons in his hand. He was scribbling on the white bedroom wall. I asked him if he had drawn the pictures on the wall without asking me. I hoped he would do me proud with an honest answer. Except he didn't. And my heart sank. Your child's first lie is bound to happen, but it is, nonetheless, a jarring moment.

I lied as a little kid, too. Mom forbade me to ride on the handlebars of my brother's bike because it wasn't safe. But one day I defied her. Albert rode his bike, and I balanced on the handle bars. I was wearing my little ballet tutu. I fell off and ripped my ballet tights. I had to invent a lie for Mom about what happened—I am not exactly sure what I told her, but I did it because she wouldn't like knowing I had disobeyed her.

Yes, kids do lie. Much like us adults, one of the main reasons children lie is to protect themselves. They assume, often with good reason, that telling the truth is going to get them in trouble, because they've done something that will make us angry or disappointed. And we may inadvertently encourage a child to lie by having an accusatory attitude. We have to tone down our reactions and approach the situation in a spirit of gentle correction.

But the more children get away with lying, the more they're likely to do it again, which can lead to bigger troubles, like cheating and stealing. So if you think it's happening, step in—gently and wisely. I try to help my kids learn from their mistakes in an atmosphere of trust, without cornering or confronting. I invite them to tell me what they know happened, and if they wish they had made a different choice, to tell me about that too. I try not to be accusing or judgmental, so my kids don't get defensive. All of this is harder than it sounds, but it always works better and feels better in the end.

Oba and I try to overflow with praise. When our children do something good or right, we let them know we've noticed. Our goal is to help them feel good about themselves.

Oba and I don't ignore bad behavior but, rather, call attention to it in a way that builds them up. Example: When my son Monty comes home with a "red light," meaning he misbehaved or talked too much in school, I say to him, "I know you can do better. I don't believe that was the real you." With each child and with every effort, we have to expect success while always realizing that failures will occur. The real key is to learn from the failures. Our children need us, and they need to see us as the guiding force in their lives. And we must believe in them.

Older siblings have an important role. They set an example for their younger brothers or sisters. When I was around six, one of my favorite sports was T-ball. I loved it. And I learned it from my older brother Albert. "My big bro, he knows how to play," I told myself. "So I'm going to listen to him, and what he says, goes." I remember studying that little ball on the tee and thinking only about the task at hand. "Put your focus on that ball," Albert said. "Don't let Mom or Ira or even me cheering in the stands distract you. Focus. And put that bat on the ball . . ." Even as young as I was, I knew I could learn from the skills and knowledge of someone older.

Albert knew how to behave and set an example. That's how I hope Monty will be with Amir. Anything Monty does, Amir wants to do. Once Monty sneaked a piece of candy and told Amir it was okay, I had to correct him gently by reminding him that he is the big brother who sets the example, and that is a special gift he has.

I volunteer at a middle school in Austin in a tougher neighborhood. Once I took Monty with me to see a different slice of life. Kids shoved other kids around. They banged on lockers. They talked back to their teachers. Monty watched quietly. On the way home, he said, "Mommy, those kids need discipline."

I was so proud of him.

Monty is a giver, and I'm proud of that too. At Halloween, he gives half of his candy to families who are less fortunate and need food, and he loves doing it.

I am grateful and thankful that our family is so filled with positive role models—family members and friends who are genuinely interested in our children's welfare. The role of grandparents in the lives of children is crucial. Our children spend a lot of time during the summer and school breaks with their grandparents, who influence them in positive ways.

I want to pass on my faith to my children, and I struggle with how. The question gnaws at us daily. Oba and I have decided that the best approach is to actively practice our faith with our children. They have to see us doing things like attending church, reading our Bibles, and participating in church activities. Leading them to faith by our example is one of the most important things that we can do for our children. We try to make our faith and its practice a positive thing for our children.

Kids have to see us doing the things that we expect of them. We are a churchgoing family, and my children attend Sunday school. Because they already take an active role in these things, it is becoming a big part of who they area. Oba and I feel this helps pass along important values. But whether or not church is part of your weekly schedule, I believe children need to develop an appreciation for the spiritual side of life. This doesn't have to be church or formal religion. It could be a connection with the natural world, like seeing a puppy being born, growing a little garden, or watching a beautiful sunset.

We pray with our kids, and we pray a lot. I want them to hear our wishes for them being spoken to God. This is also a great opportunity for us to teach them how to pray as they develop their own relationship with God.

It is gratifying to see children embrace faith, like when Monty helps Amir with his prayers. Kids have the power of pure belief, unshaken by doubts nor tarnished by uncertainty. Kids, if anything, help us to understand the wonder of everyday life because they are so trusting and so in awe of the little things we adults take for granted.

When I see my children pray, when I see their faith begin to sprout, I believe all the more.

I'm sure as my kids get older, I won't agree with all their choices. But at least I have comfort in knowing that I did my best to teach them to do the right thing, make the best choices, and realize that with those choices, there come consequences. As each one of our children learns life's tough lessons, we'll continue to be there for them and offer them love, support, guidance, and our prayers.

CHAPTER 12

PUTTING LIFE BACK TOGETHER

My prison time was winding down. I had grown accustomed to the dull, daily rhythm of life in a maze of wood, cinder block, and steel. I knew when to eat, sleep, work, exercise, read, and write. I knew the guards who followed the rule book religiously and those who bent it. I knew the system, what to do, who to talk to, and who not to talk to. I knew how to get by, mainly by gearing myself to the positive, not stagnating, and not allowing the routine and familiarity to dim my sense of wonder or destroy my capacity for hope.

There were days when screeching profanities broke the rhythm. Women in prison spoke about this "broad" and that "broad" like there was no tomorrow. They laughed about this lady's tits and that woman's ass. The f-word rolled off their tongues with ease and frequency. Sure, most of us have probably cussed at least once or twice in our lives. I can think of a few people who have never cussed, and I can think of a few, maybe more, who have cussed up a storm—

sometimes even a hurricane. I never got used to the profanities in prison, though.

I kept track of the days I spent in prison; I concentrated on the passage of time, however ponderous. Time went by faster when I kept busy, which was tough to do in prison. Towards the end of my sentence, I set my sights on tiny daily goals to get me through the final days. One day, a goal might be to get clean socks and T-shirts; the next day, to wash my hair. Every day, another goal: do Pilates, write a letter, finish a book, or read the newspaper. Those little goals, as inconsequential as they might sound, gave me structure, purpose, and direction. Yes, larger, long-term goals are necessary, but we all need these shorter, "pick me up" goals along the way to keep us moving forward.

Over and over again, I'd read one of my favorite psalms in the Bible: Psalm 139. It's about how God knows us, how He is with us, and how we can have a personal relationship with Him.

In Psalm 139 lie the familiar verses: "For you created my inmost being; you knit me together in my mother's womb. I praise you because I am fearfully and wonderfully made" (verses 13–14, NIV). These verses teach me that I'm no accident. My birth was divinely planned. I'm priceless because God doesn't make junk.

Psalm 139 also teaches me that I need to start looking at myself through the loving, transformative eyes of God, and that no matter what I do or where I go, I am never far from God's comforting presence.

Toward the end of my sentence, Maria Shriver, the first lady of

California, tried to visit me at Carswell. She wanted me to speak at a women's conference after my release. But the warden turned down her request for a visit. The prison's reasoning was that Maria and I had never physically met. I viewed the denial as a way for the prison to make life as difficult for me as possible.

My release date was set for August 19, 2008—two weeks shy of the full six months. I was to serve the rest of my sentence at a halfway house.

Two weeks prior to my release, my fellow inmates threw me a farewell party. It was a ritual I had participated in many times before, to celebrate the release of other inmates.

For my party, one of the ladies made me my favorite dessert, banana pudding; another one baked me a cheesecake. They also made pizza out of tortillas and a potato log, a delicious concoction of potato chips, veggies, and meat—a meatloaf of sorts.

The party was held in the prison courtyard. I received homemade cards, beautiful little bracelets, and other gifts crafted resourcefully from whatever someone could get from the commissary. One of the ladies crocheted me two blankets: one with Monty's name on it, the other with Amir's name.

On the day I was released, another one of the ladies treated me to getting my hair done in the salon. All prettied up, I got to put on the clothes sent to me by Oba—a green V-neck shirt and black Capri pants. No one had ever seen me in anything but prison-issue clothes. There was an upbeat chorus of "ahhs" and "oohs" from everyone.

When the day came, I signed some papers and was handed the few dollars I had earned during my jail time.

I waved goodbye to some of the guards, strutted the last few yards to the prison's front door, and stepped out into the muggy summer day—a world that was brighter and not regulated by locked doors and humdrum routine.

Sweat began to settle on my face, but I didn't pause to wipe it off. As quickly as my brown sandals would permit, I walked down the sidewalk toward my husband. At 7:55 a.m., after nearly six months locked inside, I was going home, finally.

Suddenly, behind me, dozens of women began cheering. They shouted, "You go, girl!"

I raised both arms and waved back. Then I sprinted into my husband's waiting arms. It was the best sprint I ever did.

I hugged Oba as tightly as I could, linked my fingers with his, and folded myself into our car. It was the first time I had traveled anywhere without handcuffs and leg irons. *I'm almost a free woman now*, I thought to myself.

I looked forward to simply being together with my husband, alone and uninterrupted, embracing, sharing a meal, just talking. I was ready to rebuild my life and bridge the distance between me and my family.

Of course, I'd be on probation for two full years.

Like prison, probation has dozens of rules. And if I was caught violating any one of them at any time over the next two years, I'd be in big legal trouble. On probation, there are a lot of things you're not supposed to do. For instance, you are not supposed to possess a firearm. I couldn't leave Austin without notifying my probation officer. I couldn't socialize with anyone who has a felony conviction. I couldn't do anything out of the ordinary without telling my probation officer.

My next stop was a halfway house, where I'd be in custody until September 5, 2008, in anticipation of greater freedoms that would soon be mine.

A halfway house, technically, is a place for people like drug addicts or pushers, those with mental health issues, or people with tough criminal records. Its purpose is to help them transition successfully back into society and find jobs. A person can work in the community during the day and return to the "house" at night, where they participate in other programs and undergo intense supervision. Did that profile fit me? No. I wouldn't be going out on interviews. I didn't need to be retrained or supervised. It was a waste of taxpayer dollars to board someone like me in a halfway house.

The halfway house to which I was assigned was in Austin. I was happy about that, because at least I'd be close to my house.

After we pulled up and I checked in, the officials there couldn't find my name and information. It took awhile before they realized there was a mix-up and that I had reported to the wrong facility. Once that was cleared up, we were sent to the correct halfway house.

We drove up to that halfway house. It looked like a vermin-infested, derelict building, a grim, blighted apartment building. It was one of the darkest corners of the human condition. My heart sank and my spirit died.

Men were housed on one side, women on the other. A courtyard divided the two areas. It was in the courtyard where people congregated to smoke. Every time you'd open the door to the women's side, a huge gust of cigarette smoke would blast inside. It was disgusting. I held my breath, trying not to inhale the foulness, and dashed away from the cloud of sick smoke.

There were about fifteen women and hundreds of men. The men and women were not supposed talk or fraternize with each other. Keep in mind, these men hadn't been around women in years. They gawked, leered, and hissed like they wanted a piece of us. The experience was nerve shattering.

There were no trained security guards—just normal, inexpert volunteers—so this behavior was not policed. I immediately felt threatened and didn't feel like this situation should be dismissed so easily. These episodes may not constitute abuse per se, but they certainly feel abusive to the women who have to live through them.

I had some real concerns about the environment. I thought it was unsafe, unsanitary, and threatening. I just couldn't stay silent in the face of injustice. Staying silent when you know you should speak up has repercussions. You begin mistrusting your own judgment. You ignore the powerful weapon of your own intuition. You don't listen to your gut. All of this can lead to even bigger trouble—like poor decision making and bad judgment.

I requested a meeting with my probation officer to register my concerns. She just threw up her hands. "This place is where the court wants you. You'll have to just wait it out."

It was going to take all of my energy to do that. I would have much rather stayed at Carswell the remaining two weeks of my sentence than at this place. Can you believe I said that? Yes, the halfway house was that bad. Even now, to remember that place would be to invoke nightmares.

Fortunately, there was a little gym where I could work out. It had a good rule: if there was a female in the gym, a man couldn't come in and vice versa.

I didn't eat meals in the halfway house cafeteria, because I didn't want to have to sit among those men. It wasn't because I felt better than anyone else; it was just that I didn't feel safe. I bought Hot Pockets from a vending machine and microwaved them for meals. They sustained me.

I slept in a room by myself. It had a bunk bed and some towel racks. The bathroom was outside the room and served several of the rooms, like a college dormitory bathroom.

I was allotted two hours a day to leave the premises. I used that time to go to church, to the shopping center, or to my house. On one of my first trips home, I retrieved some sheets, pillows, and towels, because the linens and bedding supplied by the halfway house were old and ragged. I didn't know where they had been or how they might have been used.

On the day of my release from the halfway house, my bags were packed and at the door. I was set free at midnight. At 12:01 I was out the door and headed home. Oba and I stopped at the Waffle House, because I was so hungry. Waffles never tasted so good, and I don't even like waffles that much.

Days later, Oba and I headed to the Austin airport to be reunited with Monty and Amir. It had been six months, but it seemed like six years.

I have been in hundreds of airports during my life. They are the place of so many of our most significant comings and goings. Hugs of joy, hugs of welcome, hugs of I'll-miss-you-so-much. They all happen at airports, maybe more so than at any other type of public building. When I'd fly to events, I'd always notice the eager eyes in the crowd at the gate, eyes searching for someone special to arrive. I'd see the tender scene of grandparents giving their grandchildren a final hug goodbye, trying to keep from crying as the little ones are flown off to a distant home. My heart would soften at seeing a boyfriend with a beautiful bouquet of flowers awaiting the moment his long-distance girlfriend stepped off the plane. Now it was my turn to stand among men and young women, anxious aunties and uncles, grandpas, grandmas, tots, wives, husbands, boyfriends, and girlfriends waiting in the airport to welcome home their loved ones.

That was the happiest day of my life, far happier than winning a medal or walking out of prison. It was the day I would be reunited with my boys.

I wrung my hands, clutched a tissue, and scanned every face coming off of the plane. I couldn't wait to give my babies kisses and cuddles again. I just wanted to hold them in my arms and tell them how much I love them. I had imagined this day so many times. I couldn't even believe it was happening.

After a few tense moments, my emotions burst into joy. Out clambered a tearful but grinning Monty, with little Amir behind him, being pushed in a stroller by my father-in-law. Monty ran straight into my awaiting arms. Amir was very quiet and overwhelmed. We all just hugged each other. I was so overcome and just said, "My boys, my boys," over and over again.

What we did as a family was go home, reconnect, put everything behind us, and start new. We moved forward, I had to partition my days into manageable chunks—one hour at a time, if need be. During each hour, I found something to enjoy and be thankful for, such as the way my children played with their favorite toys or tussled with our chow, Izzy. There is transforming joy in the simplest things.

I always knew that I wanted to have more than two children—maybe even four or five—so when I found out I was pregnant again, it was a joyous, welcome discovery. I was sure that I would have another boy—plus, we have all the clothes for boys—so it just made sense that God would bless us with another son.

Imagine our surprise when up on the ultrasound screen came the image of a baby girl. We were speechless—like two deer caught in the headlights.

Oba and I were so surprised that we asked the technician to re-check the ultrasound.

Sure enough, we were having a girl.

Oba couldn't contain his joy.

Eva-Marie started coming into the world without a nurse or doc-tor in the birthing room. The nurse had stepped out to arrange for me to have some blood work, when all of a sudden, I screamed to Oba, "She's starting to come out. We need to push! Get the nurse!" I was in a great deal of pain; I had asked for an epidural but the nurse misunderstood my request and didn't think I wanted one.

Oba got very nervous and dialed the wrong number. He darted out the room and into the hallway and started yelling for help.

Everything worked out wonderfully. Eva-Marie was born healthy and beautiful, on Monty's birthday, June 28. She is named for my grandmother and Oba's great grandmother (Eva) and one of his aunts (Marie).

The next day Monty and Amir saw their new little sister for the first time. Their faces just lit up like it was Christmas—they immedi-ately took pride in knowing that they had a baby sister and they were looking forward to the responsibility of looking after her.

For Monty, Eva-Marie was the best birthday present ever.

He leaned over, looked at her sleeping eyes, and said, "You and I will always have this special day together."

At home with my husband and three children, I felt as content and happy as I had ever been, despite the harsh reality that I was no longer an Olympic athlete and virtually penniless.

My most immediate challenge was financial. I was once a millionaire. Now I was broke. I faced a mountain of debt and legal fees. The bank had foreclosed on my home in Chapel Hill, North Carolina. I had lost almost everything I had worked so hard to achieve.

Losing everything had a huge impact on my family's life. I knew we had to change our whole lifestyle and downsize everything. We tackled this from a practical and spiritual standpoint and started to rethink what was most important to us.

Practically, we started making a lot of little changes, many of which we should have been doing anyway. We were more careful about turning off the lights. I didn't buy expensive premium foods anymore; I shopped at bulk stores like Sam's Club and I got more serious about using coupons. It felt healthy to tell my children "no" at the store; I think that was an important lesson for them to learn. We don't eat out a lot. We figured out where we were spending and where we could save the most. We began doing things ourselves around the house to save on repairs. Oba turned into a great Mr. Fix-It. When feasible, we took road trips to places rather than fly. It might seem like these changes were too little to matter, but I was amazed by the amount of money we started saving, even if it was five dollars here or ten dollars there.

We didn't obsess about our finances all the time. Had we done that, we'd be curled up in a ball in the corner all day. What the money makeover taught me was to take one day at a time and turn to Scriptures like: "And my God will meet all your needs according to his glorious riches in Christ Jesus" (Philippians 4:19). When you believe that, the future begins to take care of itself.

I didn't know when things would get better. But because of this challenge, I realized how strong we are as a family, that we are capable of pulling together when times are hard.

Oba and I learned to wait on God to release us, to restore us, and to bring us to a place of financial peace. We knew that when we didn't include God in our daily lives, we engaged in self-made decisions, quick solutions, and instant answers. What we'd end up doing was creating a bigger mess, making the situation worse.

While God did His part, I knew I had to do mine. My part was to figure out what I call my "it factor"—that inner potential that is the key to self-confidence, success, and fulfillment. Everyone has an "it factor." It's a bundle of our strengths, talents, and gifts—everything we offer to the world. I had to sit down and identify mine to get a greater vision of what was possible.

I asked myself a lot of questions: What would I love to do? What makes me happy? What are my talents? Where could I use them? I decided that I loved working with kids—so maybe I could talk to children in schools or become a coach of some sort, helping people live a champion life. I may not be an Olympian anymore, but I have the focus and motivation of an Olympian.

Olympians believe in their dreams, so I let myself dream again and have goals. Focus always precedes success, so I like to dream without distraction. I like to set goals that are just out of reach, but not out of sight—like five medals in a single Olympics. Why? So I can always get better. I like to pick something lofty that I want but don't have yet and ramp it up. This is the essence of champion living.

I believe that all of us can be champions. The word itself originates from the Latin *campus*, meaning "field," as in a battlefield or playing field. By definition, a champion is one who gains possession of a particular field. The number of fields up for grabs is limited only by our imagination and willingness to persist. Our fields can be anything from becoming a published writer to running a marathon. And winning doesn't have to mean crossing the finish line first but simply trying our hardest and meeting our goals, one by one.

Being faced with life challenges is the perfect time to recreate our lives, because it forces us out of our rut. Far too many people stay stuck in ruts because, although there's not a lot of pleasure, there's not a lot of pain either. It might just be time to climb out of your rut and go where no part of you has gone before.

Be courageous enough to risk it. Courage is not a feeling; it is an action. Real courage is pushing forward even when we experience a setback or a failure. Failure is a natural consequence of trying. We can learn from failure rather than make excuses for it. Failure can actually challenge us to new heights of accomplishment.

With a strong belief in ourselves, we can cultivate our talents. Talent is something we're born with, given to us at the moment we were conceived. It could be the ability to use a paintbrush to create amazing art or write a symphony or run fast, like me.

My job—and yours—is to dust off and uncover those talents so they can bud and blossom. At thirty-four, I've still got it in me to compete, so maybe there are other sports I can pursue. I'm also pretty good at communications. Maybe I could redirect the energy I had put into track and field toward motivational speaking.

The world needs innovative, resourceful, and creative people, and we all have our own strengths and talents to offer. We just have to figure out our "it factor" and how to make it work for us.

It certainly took me a while to wade through the wreckage I had created, but eventually things fell into place. God began to slowly turn our fortunes around. One day we looked around, and things were changing. Suddenly, what we had been praying for, what we had been waiting for was here, and it seemed that everything began to fall in place: opportunities to play professional sports, do speaking engagements, and appear on television.

I believe that one good thing leads to another. Get together a plan in which you are dedicated to achieving your dreams and goals. Do anything to keep your momentum going forward. You'll be amazed at what can happen. You get the promotion, the job comes, your marriage is restored, the doctor says the test is negative, and you find yourself saying, "I just can't believe it!" Then call your friends and family and say, "Let me tell you how God has answered my prayers!"

To endure tough times, I have learned to pray and turn my troubles over to God. I keep believing with all my heart, mind, and soul that "this too shall pass." I focus on every bit of good that comes my way. Life for me may never get back to normal. I'll never forget what happened. And that's good, because then I can remember how far I've come.

CHAPTER 13

TAKE A BREAK

Hundreds of students filed into the high school auditorium for my "Take a Break" talk. The presentation, which I have given at several high schools since my release from prison, is my attempt to encourage kids to learn from my mistake of lying and to "take a break," think, and get proper advice from those people in your life whom you trust before making impulsive decisions—about drugs, about relationships, about anything that could mess up their lives.

I start by entertaining them with my glory stories—racing against the greats, meeting presidents, or being on the *Tonight Show*—to get their attention before I get serious.

"I'm the one who took a performance-enhancing drug. I'm the one who decided to lie about it because I was trying to avoid certain consequences," I tell the crowd. "I was like a kid who spills juice on the carpet. In an effort to cover my mess, I tried to wipe up the accident and ended up rubbing the stain in and spreading it out. As a result, I lost my reputation and I suffered public humiliation, and I eventually lost my freedom."

I don't mince words. I tell them, "I made a mistake. When confronted with the truth, I decided to lie. Don't do what I did."

I hope that young athletes, in particular, will realize all this, and because of my example, decide not to go down that path.

I share with the kids that critical moment when I was interviewed by federal agents, realized that in fact I had taken "the clear," then decided to lie about my use of a steroid and my knowledge of a check I endorsed and my boyfriend's involvement in a check fraud scheme. I'm open with them about how those bad decisions tore down everything I had had built: relationships, championships, everything. Many people can't trace a turning point in their lives to one moment, but I can.

If only I had taken a break, used thirty seconds to think and make a wiser decision . . . if only I had consulted with an adviser . . . if only I had gone to the bathroom and thought this through, then things would have been a lot different.

From time to time, we all get a touch of the "if only's," but bad cases can sideline us for a long while. We think: if only I hadn't missed this; if only I'd spent more time on that; if only I'd saved more money. Or in my case, if only I had taken a break in that San Jose conference room to listen to my attorneys and get the right advice.

Well, one thing is certain—we can't change the past, but we can mold the future. We've got to play the hand we're dealt—or in some cases, the hand we deal ourselves—and make the best out of what we have. We have to use the resources available to us, whatever they are, big or small.

The more I thought about the "if only's" and reflected on the hard lessons I've learned, the more I realized that I could help people positively alter events in their lives. I don't want any young person to wait until they're thirty-four years old or older to figure out how things could have been better. I want them to figure it out now!

So the whole idea of "Take a Break" stems partly from my chronic case of those "if only's." But I chose to back off from the defeatist possibilities of the "if only's" and turn my soul searching into something constructive, and "Take a Break" was born. Sure, I could have found a quiet place and stayed away from the scrutiny and all the questions about my bad decisions. But I made the choice not to disappear, not to crawl up in a hole, not to be a hermit, but to put myself out there and hopefully help people change their lives.

One of my messages is: If we really should have done something differently to have a better result, let's learn from the situation. Make sure we know what we did poorly. Adjust our responses. And then do better the next time.

And so, I advise kids to think about what they've got planned. Is there anything that has the potential for regret later? Is there anything they know they should spend more time on? If we do each task, each job, thoroughly and well the first time, we'll have fewer regrets. We can look back and say, "I did my best."

It took me awhile to find a cure for my "if only's," but I did. I no longer spend time letting regrets flit through my thoughts. I found that it's better to fill my mind with "I'm so happy's."

I'm so happy I like to read, for example. I'm happy for the Bible and all the inspirational books I read while in prison. I'm happy for those authors whose insights enrich my own.

I'm so happy for all the times that I chased after my dreams. I was able to compete in the Olympics, travel around the world, and experience different cultures.

I'm happy that I've been able to travel to Belize, my mother's native country. I fell in love with my family there and the country. I felt a strong affinity to the Belizean culture and people. I loved the smell of the lush vegetation, the trees and the fruits, and the sight of brightly colored clothes hung on lines.

I'm happy that my three children are as different as night and day. Monty is high-spirited. Amir is laid-back and a natural jokester who loves to laugh. Eva-Marie is delicate but tough because she has to inch herself out of the way of her brothers' rowdiness. All three are a wonder to behold.

I'm happy that my own mother gave me opportunities to explore my gifts and strengths by letting me participate in all kinds of activities, from soccer to ballet to just hanging out with friends.

I'm happy that Oba is such a man of faith. My own faith was never very strong until I met him, and I wasn't a churchgoer. It was Oba who called me out of the shell I had built around myself to keep God out. I didn't think I was good enough for God because of all the mistakes I had made. I was like the centurion in the Bible who said, "No way, Jesus, you can't come in my house. I'm not worthy." But Oba taught me that God loves us and loves us without condition.

Oh—and this one: I'm happy that the courage to speak the truth finally found me. I never thought I would say that, but I really am. Who and what I am now would not be possible had I not admitted my lies, embraced the truth, and walked through all that I have.

I sure haven't used up all my "I'm so happy's" by any means. I'm so happy that I can dream again. They're not the same dreams as before, but they are just as important. I dream of my baby daughter's first steps, of going to my kids' sporting events someday, and of seeing them graduate from school and college.

I talk to young people about all of the good they can have in their lives, as well as the bad—such as hanging around with questionable people, like I did. Now, as I rebuild my own life, I see more than ever the importance of keeping good people in your corner all the time. Sometimes you need to step back and look at who you associate with and decide if their influence on you is right or best for your life. Sometimes you have to separate yourself from your friends for a while. Hopefully they'll realize that if they want to hang around with you, they can't smoke or do drugs. They have to respect how you feel and what makes you comfortable—that's what a friend is. If they don't respect your feelings, you don't need to be hanging out with them. Choose to be true to yourself, that's what I tell kids.

All children will feel the pull of peer pressure from time to time, when "all their friends" do or own things that their parents are against. As parents, we need to listen to our children and know who their friends are. We need to keep repeating that smoking and drinking aren't okay. We've got to set the rules and the boundaries. And if you don't want your children to say it, do it, or think it, you had better not say it, do it, or think it!

I also encourage kids to take a stand. There's a famous saying: *If you don't stand for something, you'll fall for anything.* This is so very true.

It's important that we figure out what we believe in so we can stand for it. Long before we have to make a decision, we've got to think about our values—those deeply held beliefs that guide our actions. For example, if kids value their athletic skills, they may say "no" to smoking cigarettes or marijuana. Each one of us has unique values that influence our decisions. So how do you figure out your values? Ask yourself questions like: Whom or what do I care about? What holds meaning for me? What are the beliefs I won't budge on? What qualities do I respect in people I admire?

But there's a flip side. Sometimes, standing up for something may make us unpopular or uncool. It may strain some relationships or cause us to lose friends. It may even bring us attention that we don't wish for. And, honestly, no one wants any of these, which is why we often go along with the crowd. But, sometimes we have to take a break to stand up for what we know is right and best for us.

Sometimes we have to say, "I'm not doing this regardless of who else is!" and set boundaries that we won't cross. And although in the short run we may feel lonely, rejected, or ashamed because of our decisions, standing up usually pays off in the long-run.

We admire those who stand up against injustice or hatred when others won't. Think of people in history who took a stand and made the world a different place. Institutionalized injustice prompted Rosa Parks to take a stand that helped African Americans gain equal rights. She believed that having to give up her seat on a bus because she was black wasn't right. Another person who took a stand was the apostle Paul. His conversion on the road to Damascus transformed him into a dynamic force for his faith.

Any one of us can make a difference by taking a stand. We don't have to be famous. This is beautifully illustrated in the starfish story, where a young man on the beach was picking up one starfish at a time and throwing it back into the ocean. Another man came along and asked what he was doing. The young man replied that the starfish would die if he left them there. The older man joked that there was no way he'd get to all the starfish and make a difference. The young man picked up a starfish, and as he threw it back into the water, said "I made a difference to that one."

I believe we can make a difference, every day and in every moment. As soon as we walk out our front door, we set off a chain reaction in the way we smile or help someone or simply believe in them. God wants to bless someone through us. We can be a role model, a mentor, an example. He doesn't want us wandering around with no destiny, no purpose, no joy, no enthusiasm. He wants us to touch lives. It's not important if you touch one life or thousands. It's just important that you exist.

I know this now, but in the past, I did not stand up strongly against what I felt was not quite right or best for me. Sometimes, out of love, fear, shame, or misplaced loyalty, I kept quiet or didn't do all I should have to stop certain things from happening. And I eventually faced negative situations and made bad choices that I could have avoided if I had just taken a stand.

Right now, many of you are facing or going to face tough choices in your life. And the sooner you take a break and decide what you are going to stand for, the better chance you have of being strong when faced with peer pressures and the temptation to do wrong or what is not in your best interest.

One of the best decision-making tools is to get proper advice. Sometimes, we think we're too grown up or too smart or too impor-tant to listen to anyone. Or we may be too proud or hardheaded to listen to counsel. But the right advice can help dreams and ambitions become reality.

I learned this too late in life. I was just ten years old when I first met one of my idols, Jackie Joyner-Kersee. She's a former Olympian who is among the all-time greatest track and field athletes in the world. I got to shake her hand at a meet in Spokane, Washington. She was giving a talk to us kids, and I shyly asked her for an autograph.

Years later, I saw Jackie again. It was in 1997, after I had won the 100-meter and the long jump at USA Outdoor Track & Field Championship. She gave me encouragement and advice: "You have so much ahead of you," she said. "Be very, very careful whom you trust, because there are going to be a lot of people pulling you in every direction."

She was so wise. I wish I had taken her advice to heart. But there was too much of that ten-year-old in me.

Young or old, we also hesitate to ask for advice from our own family members, even though they're one of the best sources for help and counsel. There were times in my life when my mother didn't approve of relationships I was in. The guys never caught on that she felt that way, but she couldn't hide it from me. I didn't listen to her, though; I was in a rebellious phase and dug in my heels, metaphorically speaking: *Nobody can tell me who I'm going to date or marry. You don't understand them. You don't understand me.* Of course, I should have listened to her, because she was right. They were bad for me.

I also regret not listening to my big brother Albert. He is the man I consider my closest friend, besides my husband. A brother, be he younger or older, can be a devoted and supportive confidant like no other in a woman's life. He can give you advice about the mysteries of men and can be loving and supportive in a way that another woman, especially a sister, cannot be.

Like Mom, Albert had concerns about certain men in my life and wanted to protect me against losers. He'd tell me the guy might not be the best person for me. I refused to listen to him. Then I began to realize certain things about these men, like their ethics and philosophies, and those problems bothered me. I finally figured out that all along, Albert had been trying to help me see what I already knew deep down.

Take it from someone who learned the hard way: Don't dismiss the advice and life experiences of people in your family!

I want my own children to feel like they can come to me and talk about their lives—school, friendships, social life—so I think a lot about how to accomplish that. I try to listen to the little stuff they tell me, the everyday things like schoolwork, their friends, and what's for dinner. I think kids will talk to you if they know you're going to listen. If you listen to them when they're young, they'll eventually trust you enough to talk about the heavy issues like sex, relationships, and drugs when they're older. I want to be the person my children turn to when they're struggling to make the right decisions.

Kids need heroes too. With temptations like drugs and alcohol, it's important for young people to have someone to look up to in order to inspire their dreams and fuel their ambitions. Sometimes, those heroes can be right off the pages of biographies. When I was little, I liked to read stories about track greats. Their stories gave me advice and inspiration on how to be a better athlete.

One of those stories was about Glenn Cunningham, once known as the "World's Fastest Human Being," and a former world-record holder in the mile run. The amazing thing is that he did it after suffering life-threatening burns on both legs as a seven-year-old when a stove in a school classroom exploded, killing his older brother Floyd. Doctors told Glenn and his parents that he would never walk again. The doctors even wanted to amputate his legs. But his parents prayed that their son's legs would heal. He spent seven months in bed. His mother kneaded his damaged muscles every day. Eventually, Glenn would walk. Then he could run. He went from crutches to world-class runner because of persistence and determination.

So did Wilma Rudolph, another hero of mine. She shocked the world in 1960 by winning three gold medals at the Olympic Games. That was incredible, given that as a child, Rudolph was crippled with polio and shackled with leg braces that kept her from walking until age nine. She was told then by doctors she would never walk, but she proved them all wrong, battling past her infirmity to become one of the greatest women athletes in history.

Jesse Owens is a hero of mine for many reasons. At the 1936 games in Berlin, he was the first American to ever win four gold medals in a single Olympics, for the 100 meter, the 200-meter, the broad jump, and as a 100-meter relay runner. Hitler could not believe what he was seeing. In an atmosphere of anti-black Nazi propaganda, Owens's performance shattered Hitler's claim of a superior Aryan race.

Returning from the Berlin Olympics, Owens expected to be greeted as a hero. He was sadly disappointed. He received no sport endorsements, no telephone calls from high-ranking officials, not even from President Roosevelt. After months of hardship, he was reduced to running against race horses and motorcycles to make money. In the mid-1950s, Owens became involved with the Chicago Youth Commission. He spent the rest of his life traveling the country doing speeches on patriotism and religion.

I was honored to receive the Jesse Owens International Trophy four times and thus have my name linked with his. Established in 1981, the award is USA Track & Field's highest accolade and is presented annually to the outstanding male and female track and field performers. I'd always believed that it was a deep disgrace that Jesse Owens wasn't recognized as a hero while he was still in his prime, and I'm glad to see how far we've progressed since then. He inspired me to make an impact on people's lives as he did on the sport of track and field.

We need to carefully choose our heroes, advisors, and mentors. Do they inspire us to higher levels of achievement? Are they experienced? Do they have our best interests at heart? Can they give us what we need (insight into organizational culture, technical skill, and so forth)? How are they perceived? Are they respected? Does their opinion carry any weight? Have they walked in our shoes? Getting wise advice helps us make solid choices.

Then we've got to evaluate and decide. Armed with information, we must consider our options and the consequences of each. Seriously weighing our options can help guide us toward good decisions. Some tips to keep in mind: Give equal weight to your rational thoughts and your feelings. Both are important. List the pros and cons of each decision. Write them down. Seeing these on paper can make the decision easier. And don't make decisions if you're stressed out, tired, or upset. A negative state of mind might cloud your judgment.

"Everyone has a choice in life," I tell students. "It's up to you what you do with it. Think about how your parents, grandparents, brothers, and sisters would feel if you made the wrong choices and got into trouble or got sent to prison. It's a bad feeling to be locked up in a little room and not be able to get out. Open your minds and think about your choices before you act."

I like to open the floor to questions. Kids are curious about prison, particularly about the kind of food inmates get and whether prison is like what you see in movies. I tell them you lose your freedom and you can't do what you want to do. It's no fun in prison. I emphasize that if they take a break and make the right choices in life, they won't end up there.

Sometimes, I ask myself, "What if a Marion Jones came into my life at the age of thirteen and spoke to me and shared her story? Would that have made a positive difference in my life?" Possibly, probably.

I take my new role and my impact in these Take a Break talks very seriously, which is why it's important for me to tell my story my way. I've matured even more since I've been out of prison, and my life has become so much more complete and centered. I want young people everywhere to relate to me and my experiences, so they can identify with what I've been through and walk a straight, honest path toward lifelong success.

As my talk winds down, I ask the kids: What are you going to do when you feel full of self-doubt, fragile, or alone?

"Take a break!" they shout.

When you're facing tough choices? "Take a break!"

When you need advice? "Take a break!"

When you're deciding who to hang out with? "Take a break!"

I'm happy about something else: the kids are in sync with my message. They know to stop, step away, and take a break.

CHAPTER 14

THE SHOCK

It was a crisp warm day in April 2010, and I had some dirty work in front of me: washing cars in a parking lot. I'd start on the top of a car, work my way down with a large soapy sponge, and then try to keep the just-washed areas properly hosed so the soap wouldn't dry on them. Washing cars wasn't for fun or profit or getting wet. It was a ritual—all part of being a rookie for the WNBA's Tulsa Shock—and the oldest one ever in the history of the league.

With the Shock, rookie hazing is a tradition. Rookies are routinely asked to perform menial tasks such as carrying everyone's bags on the road, buying sandwiches for all the players before practice, and gathering up balls that are purposely thrown into the stands.

I didn't mind. I was just glad and grateful to be playing for Tulsa.

My journey to Tulsa began in May 2009. Out of the blue, I got a text message from a friend with strong ties to the NBA and WNBA. The text said, "Marion, would you be interested in playing in the WNBA?"

Eight months pregnant with my daughter, I laughed at the prospect of playing pro *anything*. "LOL," I texted back.

My friend wrote: "No, this is serious. There is interest in the WNBA."

I sat down and talked it over with Oba. We took our own break. We weighed the positives and the negatives, the pros and the cons. On one hand, I wasn't sure I wanted me and my family to be back in the glare of public scrutiny. And I loved being a wife and a mom. Playing professional sports would mean a nomadic lifestyle and leaving my kids again.

On the other hand, I realized I had an unquenched competitive drive to play sports again. I missed the training; I missed the competition; I missed everything related to it. I was further fueled by the thought that a lot of people probably wouldn't think I could do it. I'm the type of person who loves a challenge.

Oba and I prayed about it together, with our pastor, and with members of our church.

It was a tough decision for us, but we decided to go for it. There is a scene in the movie *Chariots of Fire* when young Harold Abrahams, a champion sprinter, has just lost his first race. He sits alone, pouting in the bleachers. His girlfriend tries to encourage him, but he mourns, "If I can't win, I won't run!" To which she wisely responds: "If you don't run, you can't win." Abrahams went on to win the 1924 Olympic Gold Medal in the 100-meter run.

And so Oba and I decided that this could be a win-win for everyone. We reminded ourselves that we would be doing it for the good of the entire family. Most of all, we reasoned, it might be a way to promote my Take a Break program.

There was no second guessing; we were confident about our decision. The next step was to meet with the president of the WNBA, Donna Orender. I wanted to share with her my desire to play basketball. I wanted the league to know that I had the passion and ability to play at the highest level . . . and the WNBA is "the" premier women's professional basketball league in the world! I also wanted to know that I had the WNBA's support.

The WNBA's interest in me and my interest in them must have been destiny. Being a women's basketball fan, I was watching Sports-Center one day in 2003 when I was pregnant with Monty. The sports-caster announced a "Marion Jones" drafted to the Phoenix Mercury. "Cute," I thought. "There's a player with my name." But when he said she was from North Carolina and then my manager called to tell me I'd been drafted, I realized they were talking about me. *That's surreal*, I thought. I wasn't even running that year and hadn't played basketball since 1997. I guess it was some kind of sign.

The meeting with the WNBA in 2009 was encouraging. I was welcomed with open arms but reminded that making a team would not be easy. The WNBA is very competitive. Each team is allowed only eleven players, whereas NBA teams have fourteen or fifteen—so there just aren't many slots available for women pros. Donna reminded me, too, that today's WNBA players are the best in the world. I decided to use that admonition as a source of motivation for myself.

I was excited but knew that I had to get in basketball shape soon and regain my court instincts. Those instincts, though now rusty, had taken hold back when I was in elementary school. Mom enrolled me in a private school called Pinecrest and worked long hours for a Beverly Hills law firm to pay for it. I used to mess around shooting hoops, but Pinecrest had a whole program, run by my first real coach, Geoff Jarvis. I quickly made the team since I'd developed rudimentary skills by playing with boys on the courts at recess.

Basketball became much more important to me after Mom and I decided I should attend college on a basketball scholarship instead of track. I'd started receiving letters from colleges at the beginning of my freshman year. By the end of my senior year, I'd gotten four hundred. I was attending Thousand Oaks High School then, a school very well known in the California basketball world. We were always nationally ranked, and I learned heaps and heaps about the game.

I didn't really consider the University of North Carolina until Mom told me a story: when she was a little girl living in Belize and her friends asked her where she wanted to live when she grew up, she's always tell them "North Carolina." And it somehow stuck in her mind that she'd live there one day.

As I reflect on that story today, I see within it the power of having a vision. A vision is twofold: a picture of exactly what you want to do or have and a picture of yourself already doing it or having it. A vision clarifies your goals and serves as a constant reminder and motivation to keep working toward them. It reminds you why you get up in the morning.

Anyway, after Mom told me that, I started reading about the university and soon found myself getting very interested in its communications program and in its basketball program. They flew Mom and me to Chapel Hill. It was love at first sight. The campus was gorgeous; the people were welcoming and warm. I felt at home there. It was where I belonged, and I accepted their basketball scholarship.

Now, it was thirteen years since those college days. I was unfit and heavy—179 pounds as opposed to my normal weight of 149—because I had just given birth to Eva-Marie. I knew the game wasn't the way I left it. The game was ten times faster, and the athletes were ten times more skilled. I would need a good coach who could help me learn and relearn the skills that are relevant to today's style of play.

I hired Olaf Lange, one of the assistant coaches for the WNBA's San Antonio Silver Stars, and Tonya Holley, the head trainer for the Stars. Olaf is a no-nonsense guy from Berlin with an impressive résumé of coaching credentials; Tonya, a fit, kind-spirited woman with a perpetually wide grin. Both knew the sport, and they knew what the WNBA coaches were looking for.

In September 2009, my new race was on; the finish line: a superbly conditioned body worthy of playing professional basketball with the best. Olaf gave me a brutal training routine to do the first month. I'd head to a community center in Austin every day to train. The place was a haven of energy for hard work. Brown brick walls, no swanky juice bars. The air inside was thick, moist. Iron clanged. Stationary bikes vroomed. I'd run on high-speed treadmills. I'd lift weights. I'd shoot basketballs just to get the feel of the ball. It wasn't just exercising. It was sweat and sacrifice. After a couple of hours, perspiration was dripping off every part of my body. It was hard work, but I loved it.

In October, I began making the commute to San Antonio three times a week to train with Olaf and Tonya for three to four hours. The other two days a week, I'd keep up with my conditioning in Austin. Those days, I'd have to be out of the gym by 1:15 in the afternoon so I could pick my boys up from school by 3:00. I wasn't just dribbling; I was juggling.

From the beginning, Olaf told me that he wanted me to work hard and do a lot of extra drills and workouts to get back to where I used to be. I had to relearn how to shoot, even how to dribble.

Ball handling was never my strength in college; my speed on the court made up for the deficit. I needed to correct my sloppy skills, but I also needed to learn today's method of ball handling. In college, we were taught to squeeze the ball with our fingertips and keep it low to the court. Nowadays, you've got to dribble the ball higher and pound it harder.

There were drills—lots of drills. Tough, exhausting ones. I'd stand in place and pound the ball with my left hand. I'd walk down court, pounding the ball. Then, I'd dribble the ball between my legs, down the court and back. I'd dribble two balls at the same time. I'd practice jump shots, passing shots, layups, and rapid-fire shots from anywhere on the floor to simulate game conditions. I'm a perfectionist, so I'd practice over and over and over and over again.

Fortunately, breaks were a part of the practice sessions. They gave me time to catch my breath and wipe the beads of sweat off my face.

Playing the game was like riding a bike—once mastered, never forgotten. I had a strong foundation because I had been coached in college by Sylvia Hatchell, who was one of the all-time great teachers of the game. She was someone who really believed in me. I think that's vital for success. We tend to live up to the compliments we receive.

I remember the time she called me into her office after only my second day of practice.

"Marion, I want you to be a point guard for the team," she said.

"Are you sure?" Point guard is a pivotal position on a team and the de facto leader of the team. I wasn't ungrateful or nervous or anything, but my skills were underdeveloped.

"Have you seen me dribble?" I continued.

Coach Hatchell had thought long and hard about it and figured that you can always teach someone ball handling, you can always teach someone to shoot, but raw, natural speed—which you need if you're going to be a point guard—is hard to come by.

Basketball eventually all came back to me, but it took a lot of hard work and concentration.

My first tryout was scheduled in December 2009 for Brian Agler, the coach of the Seattle Storm. In the off-season, he lives in Ohio, so that's where the tryout was held. I was nervous, but confident. Brian would be watching and evaluating me. It would be his decision whether or not he wanted me. I knew that I could do only what I could control and that was to get out there, go hard, and play the best I possibly could. So that's what I did. I thought I moved fast and gracefully, dribbling toward the basket and launching shots. It felt good.

Brian told me that it was an excellent tryout. He didn't give me any idea of whether he wanted me or not, but he sent me home with some excellent advice on shooting and ball handling. He recommended that I play as many pick-up games as I could. Oba and I found some games at a middle school in Austin where there were some high-quality players who agreed to let me play.

Then disaster struck. It was January fourth. Oba and I hired a babysitter so I could go play. I was playing well, but an hour into the game, I went up for a shot, came down and landed on someone's foot, rolled my right ankle, and fell hard to the court. I couldn't get up, and I couldn't walk. Oba rushed me to a nearby emergency room. I had torn three ligaments in my right ankle.

I sat on the examination table and sobbed. My ankle was in pieces and so were my new dreams.

For seven weeks, I wore a compression boot on my ankle, underwent heavy icing, and had intense massage and ultrasound treatments. All forms of vigorous activity were put on hold. I couldn't do a thing—no training, no drills, no playing, nothing.

Fortunately, I had people on my personal team who were working tirelessly on my behalf. One was Dr. Robert Meyer, a highly sought after chiropractor and ART (Active Release Technique) specialist in Austin, Texas who treated and helped me get the ankle ready to play again. Another was my professional basketball representative, Susie Jarosch, who was trying to set up meetings for me with different coaches in the WNBA.

One of the coaches who wanted to meet me was Nolan Richardson, head coach of the Tulsa Shock.

Nolan Richardson? He was a living legend in basketball circles, a god.

I knew that Coach Richardson had a long string of firsts as a coach. In 1965, he was the first black coach in El Paso, at Bowie High School, a school he had integrated as a player. In 1980, he guided Western Texas Junior College to a national title. He became the first black junior college coach to win it all.

When he joined the University of Tulsa in 1980, Coach Richardson was the first black coach at a major college in the state of Oklahoma. And when he was hired to coach the University of Arkansas in 1986, Coach Richardson was the first black coach in the Southwestern Conference (their league then). He became the winningest basketball coach ever in Arkansas history, compiling a 389–169 record in seventeen seasons.

He had just taken the job at Arkansas when, tragically, his daughter Yvonne was diagnosed with leukemia. Yvonne Richardson died in the summer of 1987. She was just fifteen years old.

After every win, he pays tribute to Yvonne. "Baby, we got another one," he says, looking heavenward.

In February 2002, Coach Richardson claimed he was being mistreated by the Arkansas administration and fans because he was black. Arkansas soon fired him, and Richardson filed suit, which was dismissed in 2004. He was hired as head coach of the Tulsa Shock in October 2009. For the first time in his career, he'd be coaching women—and professional basketball.

I figured Coach Richardson knew something about comebacks, survival, and second chances.

His teams typically played an up-tempo game with intense pressure defense—a style that was known as "40 Minutes of Hell," also the title of his biography.

I couldn't wait to meet him. The boot still on my ankle, I flew to Tulsa in February and hobbled into the meeting.

Coach Richardson is a towering, bear-like figure with a shock of pure white hair and sleepy eyes. What first struck me was his deep voice. It might have been intimidating if not for its layers of gentleness and understanding.

I shared with him what I could bring to Tulsa: quickness, athleticism, leadership quality, and beyond all that, I could play. I didn't expect anything to be handed to me; I expected to contribute and prove I was worthy of competing in the WNBA.

"We're definitely interested," he said. "We can all talk until we're blue in the face, but we really need to see what you can do."

"As soon as I'm healed and ready, I'll fly back to Tulsa for a tryout," I said. I was thrilled.

An answer to prayer came quickly in the shape of a healthy, pain-free ankle. By the first Saturday in March, I found myself at Oral Roberts University in Tulsa, trying out in front of Coach Nolan Richardson and his staff.

This time, I was nervous. I'm used to performing in front of lots of people, but this was definitely different. And it wasn't just anyone for whom I was trying out. It was a master of the game, a coach who has seen the best of the best. I had to show him that I was skilled, committed, and passionate. The tryout lasted only an hour and fifty minutes.

Imagine my joy when Coach Richardson pulled me aside after the tryout and told me: "Watching you go through the drills, I see a player who's perfect for our system. The one thing I do know is you can run, and any player on my team who wants to be successful must be able to run. We can make this work. What you need to do is continue to practice. Work on your shots and conditioning, because with my style of basketball, you will need to be fit."

In March, I signed a one-year contract with the Tulsa Shock for $35,888.

There was a huge press conference held in Tulsa after the news broke about my signing to play in the WNBA with the Tulsa Shock. Honestly, I would have preferred to pursue this opportunity quietly, throw on my basketball shoes, and start playing. But even now, when I do things, someone insists on having a press conference.

When the Olympics came to Los Angeles in 1984 and I watched the games on TV with Ira, I was fascinated with the athletes' post-game interviews with the press—how they interacted with the journalists and how they acted, whether they won or lost. I couldn't believe that some athletes were such sore losers that they wouldn't even talk to the press afterwards if they lost. I remember telling my stepdad that when I got interviewed by the media, I would always be respectful no matter if I won or lost. And I've tried to conduct myself that way ever since.

In early May, I packed up some of my things for my temporary move to Tulsa. Monty cried and pleaded with me not to go. He bargained with me that he'd finish school three weeks ahead of time, so he could go. The tearful good-byes were all too familiar and just as heart-wrenching. Oba and I felt it was best if I lovingly tucked everyone into bed, then slipped out early the next morning before they were up.

In the weeks to come, I'd talk to my children over the webcam—usually before they went to bed, supplemented with phone calls before and after school. The first week, there was a lot of fighting and tears over camera time. What we had to do was have Monty and Amir take turns. While one of the boys played in another room, the other got to have his special time with Momma over the webcam.

I moved into a small apartment in the famed Mayo, a historic former hotel constructed in 1925 in the heart of Tulsa on a brick-lined street. Once the tallest building in the city, the fourteen-floor Mayo is supported by stately columns and decorated with lovely terra cotta balconies. It has hosted many famous people from Mae West to John F. Kennedy.

Tulsa itself is a rather intriguing city. Its skyline rises boldly from the prairie and is surrounded by gently rolling hills. In the 1920s, it became known as the "Oil Capital of the World." Although Tulsa had no oil of its own, Oklahoma was a leading oil-producing state in those days, and oil barons set up their empires in the city. Empowered by the wealth flowing into the city in the 1920s, Tulsans started building Art Deco structures. Today, Tulsa has some of the most lovingly preserved Art Deco buildings anywhere in the country.

But long before that, Tulsa was first settled by the Loachapoka and Creek Indian tribes. They proclaimed Tulsa "sacred ground."

Tulsa loves its Shock too. We're the city's only professional basketball team—there's nothing else—so we can't be overshadowed by any other team. I got to thinking: I could have made a team in some other city where WNBA basketball is unimportant. God gave me such a wonderful opportunity. I was definitely on sacred ground.

Basketball practice occasionally takes place in the BOK Center, a state-of-the-art sports and entertainment arena that seats nearly twenty thousand people. Coolers of water and Gatorade are wheeled out courtside. Bright lights are flicked on. We file out to the court, with a little friendly patter and teasing. Then Coach Richardson says, "Let's go, ladies."

We start with a series of drills that, to an onlooker, might resemble a loosely choreographed dance. We run backwards, sideways, on our toes, and on our heels. We walk, kicking up our legs, backward and forward. We skip like kids. We do wind sprints.

Then we drop to the court for a series of push-ups, reverse sit-ups, planks, and other body-challenging calisthenics.

Next, we start our practice play: layups, shooting drills, and passing drills. From there, it's on to a lot of full-court scrimmaging.

We do drill after drill after drill until we get it right. Make perfect passes; go to the next drill. Make all your layups; go to the next drill. It's go, go, go. Coach Richardson never wants us to get outworked or outhustled in games, so we work hard.

There is a pattern to our practice, and everyone falls in, lockstep and focused.

Our opening night game, May 15, 2010, was against the Minnesota Lynx at the BOK Center. It was thrilling to put on my bright yellow jersey, No. 20, everything you could possibly imagine. I felt transformed and fired up. Being on a basketball team returned a piece of myself to me.

There was a huge crowd. We ran out of the locker room through the tunnel, and we felt like Tulsa was really our city. Walking out and having the whole arena standing and clapping for us was an amazing experience. The game was on.

In the first quarter, I heard the words players love to hear: "Jones, you're in!"

I peeled off my warm-up suit and stepped on the court. I was probably the most nervous player out there, but intent on playing hard. I knew I was going to go out there and give it my all. I knew automatically I was playing for the city, for the state, for the team, for my family, and for God. I was playing for everything I stand for.

I played three minutes, nineteen seconds but did not score. Although I put forth an aggressive defense, I committed a foul three seconds after I took the floor, then allowed an opposing player to score on me seconds after that.

I was disappointed that I didn't do the right things out there. I'm a competitor, after all. As hard as I tried to play, I wanted to succeed. It's what you do. It's what you know. I want to see my team win, and I want to see myself contributing to that win.

By the time it was over, the Lynx had outshot us, in an 80–74 loss. (We clobbered them a couple of weeks later, 92–79.)

I'll say this: If a team is going to beat the Tulsa Shock, they're going to earn it. Losing is going to happen sometimes. But we can sleep well knowing that we played our hearts out.

It's not easy for me to watch from the bench while the action unfolds. I want to be out there helping us win. But I'm patient. I have every bit of confidence that I will continue to improve and that as I do, Coach Richardson will put me on the court more.

Sportswriters and commentators have speculated how well Coach Richardson's run-and-gun system would work in the WNBA. Nobody expected the Tulsa Shock to do much, really. But you should see us on the court. We pressure our opponents and force them into making turnovers. We dictate the tempo. We drive the ball and get open, precise shots. All our games are close.

Our games are exciting too. We've got catch-and-shoot forcefulness. We've got the swish, the net flipping up, the sound of the ball ripping through the twine. We're inside; we're outside. You need to play exciting basketball like that to fill up the arena. What we're doing is appreciated and fans are coming to the realization that we're not just special; we're one of the best-trained women's teams to ever step out on the court. We're competitive, exciting, and fun—and we show it every game.

Coach Richardson is always pulling us aside and pumping us up. He likes to say to the team that as long as today's practice or today's game is better than the one before, then we are going in the right direction.

Inside the locker room after games, we high-five each other or pat each other's backs for a job well done. We handle any media requests, then I take a shower.

On the way home, I think to myself, "We're a good team. A lot of teams underestimate us, but we click on all cylinders. We play with an attitude, with a lot of confidence and heart."

Our team is so diverse. We've got single players, married players, and married players like me with kids. That means we've all got different priorities. I don't go out after games; I go home and go to bed. Just because of who I am, I get more media attention. It singles me out. That's uncomfortable because I don't want to stand out; I want to fit in. I'm part of a team.

The nurturing side of women comes out in a team. We practice together; we train together; we go through everything together. We all have days when we feel down, discouraged, or just miss our families. We share our feelings with each other. These moments of truth feel like a warm blanket, and they help cultivate trust and build bonds.

At the same time, you've got to have a thick skin around your teammates. They'll speak their minds if you blow a shot or a pass. But you can't take it personally.

I admit that I was a little intimidated going in, because the other women had so much more experience that I did. They had all played basketball straight through since college. But Coach Richardson knew that and helped me get on the same page as everyone else.

And of course, I'm the oldest player on the team. Coach Richardson likes to say, "She might be thirty-four, but she has the body, the knees, the joints, and the ankles of someone much younger." He's right. Because I haven't played basketball in so long, I haven't suffered the impact and pounding experienced by some of the other players who have played continuously since high school.

With only eleven players on the team, each one of us contributes and is critical to the team. Technically, I'm a guard, but in Coach Richardson's system, players don't necessarily have specific roles in terms of positions on the team, unless of course you're very tall and can play center. But most of his players are so athletic that they can play almost any position. We're like a tool box. If Coach needs saws, we've got saws. If he needs pliers, we've got pliers. If he needs hammers, we've got hammers. You name it; our team can do it. Our versatility is what makes the Tulsa Shock unique.

We were a new team, though, with a new coach, and there are struggles. By June 2010, we were on a eight-game losing streak.

So technically, we're the underdogs now. The dictionary definition of *underdog* is someone at a disadvantage and expected to lose a contest or struggle. When you hear you're the underdog, it's not a bad thing. I think it gives you an edge, that extra bit of drive, desire, and aggression to go out there and give it your all. Whether it's David slaying Goliath or Rocky Balboa fighting his way to a win, I think we always root for the little guy.

And just because you're the underdog doesn't mean you can't win. No matter how long you've been in the game, sometimes you find yourself up against opponents who have an edge over you. Maybe they've just been around longer, have more experience, or perhaps this time, you're playing on their turf. It can either intimidate you or exhilarate you. In either case, your performance only gets stronger when you go up against people who are better than you.

The most important lesson is to not give up. You've got to keep going and moving forward, no matter what is happening around you or to you. There is power in that kind of positive thinking.

I am now more thankful than ever that before every game, we have a fifteen-minute chapel. Anyone from our team can attend. So can anyone from the rival team. The chapel is led by our team chaplain, the lean, vibrant Madeline Manning-Mims, who just happens to be the 1968 Olympic 800-meter champion at the Mexico City games. I feel blessed to be among so many legends.

In one memorable Bible study, Madeline spoke to us from the book of Esther. It describes how God placed Esther in a certain position—that of queen—so that she could save a whole nation by exposing a plot to destroy her and her people—an action that glorified God. Madeline explained to us that, much like Esther, we have been placed in a unique position, too, because of our talent and visibility. Our faith must so permeate us that everything we do will be for His glory: how we act on the court, how we play, how we talk to the media and fans, how we interact with each other and with our coach, everything. I was so moved by the teaching that I try to keep it as a guiding principle in my life by asking myself continually: Is this action glorifying God?

Basketball is like life, and life is hard sometimes. You have ups and you have downs. You have to make the right decisions at crucial moments. And you have to prepare for any obstacles you might face, and you must keep going.

Basketball has taught me the importance of dusting off discarded dreams and following them again. I figured out my "it factor." I used my skills, followed my passions, retooled myself, and chased my old dream of playing basketball.

It's been said that there are no second acts in American life, but apparently I never got the memo. I believe that anyone can rediscover an abandoned dream. Most of us carry all kinds of hopes and dreams locked away inside us. The trick is to bring them into the light of day, then examine them for relevance to our current situation. Maybe it's a hobby you can turn into a career. Maybe it's the chance to return to school and study something you've always loved. Maybe you'd like to work at home and spend more time with your children. Sit down and write a long list of things you might like to do. Give your old dreams a second chance.

■

My family joined me in Tulsa the first week in June, arriving at 2:00 in the morning after driving straight through from Austin. Tears came on like a rain that starts with a drizzle but surprisingly soon breaks into a downpour.

It was wonderful and comforting to have them with me. I was able to immerse myself in their world, take all my grown-up agendas off the table, and instead tend to their priorities. They get concerned over the littlest, teeny things like their next birthday party, their toys and games, monsters in the closet, and other three-to-six-year-old things.

I was so grateful to have them in Tulsa. I'd missed them so much. I even missed all the wonderful, little squabbles my sons have: bickering over which cartoons to watch or who gets to play games on Momma's iPhone or who started a fight.

I treasure every teachable moment I have with my children. Sure, I could try to figure out who did what to whom first. But not only is this wearisome for me, my kids learn nothing about how to get along without a referee. When they fight over which cartoons to watch, I tell them I'm confident they can work it out so everyone is happy (and if they don't, nobody watches anything). They miraculously come to an agreement.

Someone once remarked to me that the joy of parenthood starts to wane shortly after your child's second birthday. That's crazy. True, there are the tantrums, the fights, and the crying, but by two years old their true characters start to shine through and it is a total joy to watch them learn about the world.

Monty and Amir know Momma is a basketball player now, and they've watched my games on the Internet. I told my boys, "Now you get to go to the arena and see me play for real, not on TV or the computer."

Monty's eyes widened instantly.

"Do they have popcorn?"

CHAPTER 15

BLESSED

As a young track athlete, I tried hurdles but disliked them, especially after seeing people hit them and get hurt. But we've all got hurdles in life. Every so often a hurdle is much higher than I thought it would be. Then it takes a little more effort and I have to jump higher. Sometimes, the hurdle is less than I thought it would be, and I jump over it like nothing. Some hurdles you don't jump. You go around them instead. Whether you jump or go around them, you are stronger for it.

Every experience changes us in big ways and small. Being sent to prison was a transformational event in my life. It shattered my whole framework of living, and I had to glue the pieces back together, one by one. It was through the re-piecing, however, that I truly learned how to live. That hurdle—going to jail and everything that got me there—was a big one.

We will always have to jump more hurdles in life because we're constantly putting ourselves out there, going after the great things (great jobs, great relationships, a great life), and that's never risk free. And we may fall down doing it, but with faith we don't stay down. I tell myself, "This hurdle may take me down, but it's not going to take me out."

The obstacles, difficulties, and trials we experience help us grow. What happened to me was something that built my character, something I learned from, and I feel blessed because of it.

My growth process reminds me of the story of two Belizean farmers who decided to plant mango trees. One farmer hardly tended his young tree at all. It was exposed to the elements. The wind blew on it and bent its trunk, almost to the breaking point. As it grew, he let his children climb on the branches. This left nicks and cuts on the growing trunk. Yet the mango tree flourished and blossomed into a lush, spreading shade. Soon it was filled with fruits.

The other farmer overprotected his mango tree. He built a fence around it as a guard against the strong winds. He forbade his children from touching, let alone climbing, the growing tree. The trunk was unblemished. Yet, despite all his care, the mango tree was stunted. It had weak branches and sparse leaves. It bore no fruit at all.

"How can this be?" he wondered. "I pampered my tree. Why is your mango tree larger, healthier, and more fruitful than mine?"

"I don't know," answered the other farmer. "But let's ask the wise one in our village."

The wise one, who knew something about these things, told the farmers: "The winds cause the trunk and tree branches to flex so that the sap circulates and is drawn up to nourish the budding leaves. The cuts in the trunk stimulate fruiting by stifling the downward flow of water. The more swaying and stress, the stronger the tree grows."

Perhaps we need the harsh winds of life and tough breaks in the same way, though we hate enduring them. The greater the hardships, the better our character. And sometimes, blustery, rough periods in life are the prelude of new life, health, success, and happiness. In Romans 5:3–4, the apostle Paul puts it like this: "We also rejoice in our sufferings, because we know that suffering produces perseverance; perseverance, character; and character, hope" (NIV).

I hope people know by now that I am truly sorry for the mistakes that I have made. But I believe that without them I would not be the woman I am today. I've learned from the situation and determined to incorporate the lessons into other dreams and goals. As a result, I'm a different and, hopefully, a better person because of what I've been through. My life is no longer held together by ties that are already threadbare.

I now realize that I had to go down in the valley before I could look up and see the mountaintop. Yes, I prefer the clean, crisp air of a mountaintop experience, but I've learned that the valley's depth marks the mountain's height and gives it meaning.

I'm much more forgiving now too. When people disappoint me, I don't take it personally. I consider the person and realize that people are human and, like me, have weaknesses and make mistakes. I don't go around holding grudges. I don't think it serves any purpose. God serves as a role model of forgiveness. His actions toward us are a blueprint of how we should conduct our relationships with others. Whether it is the memory of my past or something that was done to me, I forgive. Forgiveness removes the barriers that hold my heart, mind, and spirit in captivity.

We certainly need people to help us get over hurdles—people who have our best interest at heart and love us unconditionally. This is so important when things become rough or rocky in our lives. The saddest people alive are those who believe they don't need anyone. The reality is that we do need people, the right people.

Life is about hurdles and the progress we make. It is about the jumping over. It's about the going around. It's about doing what's right and getting back on track.

In the many days that have passed since my incarceration, I have continued to seek a larger meaning for my life. Today, that means being the best mom and wife I can be, so that my kids are well-adjusted and have a good life. It is the summer of 2010 as I write this, and a typical day for our family starts when Monty, Amir, and Eva-Marie wake up at the crack of dawn. I love hearing their chattering in the morning. I love seeing my husband support me and being such a great dad. I love that my closest friends and family are just a phone call away.

Depending on when I have basketball practice, we go to a water park, the library, a playground, the movies, or anything fun or educational for the kids. At night, we read bedtime stories and say prayers before they go to sleep. I'm optimistic that Oba and I are raising three beautiful children who will know and understand God, will appreciate all that life has to offer, and will turn out to be three fine adults who will contribute positively to society.

Our days are what you might consider "ordinary"—days when nothing much happens. But I wouldn't trade them for the world. While I was in prison, it seemed as though a minute lasted an hour, and I couldn't wait for each day to pass. Not anymore. I treasure every single minute now, and I take every day, every experience, very slowly. I've learned that what began as ordinary can end in extraordinary blessings, like seeing Monty hug Amir after he scrapes his knee or Oba cradling Eva-Marie against his chest. Those are extraordinary blessings to me, just out of nowhere.

While in prison, I had to look hard to see any blessings. I guess that's why some blessings are called "blessings in disguise," because you can't tell they're blessings while in the middle of them. They look bad. They feel bad. So then they must be bad. Someone might be going through a really bad stretch of stuff—like a divorce, job loss, or illness—and they'll be hard-pressed to see any blessing in what's happening to them.

When something bad happens, the first thing we do is try to make sense of it. We want to know, "Why?" We wonder—at least in our minds, if not in our cries—why it is that God can allow those events, when this same God could have prevented them or changed the outcome had He determined to do so. All of these questions are very real to many of us. And when God does not perform to what I expect, why should I continue in the way of faith?

I've asked myself this question hundreds of times. All I know is that God might not always take away what we're going through, but He'll give us the resources and the strength to get through it. There is a God who says, "I'll stretch out my loving hand to you." There is a God who says, "I understand what you're going through." There is a God who says, "I know that you're hurting, but I am right here to help you in your time of need." So, although I might be having a rough time and my circumstances are not changing, I know God is in the midst, and that means blessings are coming my way.

I'm working as hard as I can for the Tulsa Shock to help the team win, whether it's by contributing to the defense while I'm on the court or being the loudest cheerleader from the bench. I'd love to have more playing time, but at the same time, I understand the situation. I knew coming into the team would be tough. I'm just trying to stay in some type of rhythm and be ready when my name is called.

Every day, I feel so blessed to be able to learn from Coach Nolan Richardson. He is an amazing coach but an even more inspiring man. The other day, before a game, when he could have been talking basketball X's and O's, he talked about the X's and O's of life. He reminded us all to be thankful for where we are right now, because there are women who would love to be in our spots and people who don't have the opportunities we have. It was a great reminder for us all about what's really important in life. Coach Richardson is a man of genuine wisdom.

No matter what happens with my basketball career, I want people to know that I always loved the game. I went to practice and to the games and played as hard as I could, and I shared it with as many people as possible. And I always enjoyed myself.

I also want to continue to speak to people around the country about my experiences and hopefully be a positive influence. I really feel that this is what this phase of my life is about: helping people make better decisions and get their lives back on track. This is so important for getting through life, because we have to make decisions every day. If we're armed in the best possible way to make them, it makes life easier. And, I tell school kids and other athletes: Make sure that what you are doing and the people you are doing it with are compatible with your beliefs. When you get an opportunity, you are going to succeed because you know to do what's right.

I am polishing my arguments for prison reform. Until 2008, I was just like everybody else when it came to prisons. I assumed they were probably the best possible way of separating the bad people from the good in what was probably a humane and rehabilitative setting. I assumed prisons deterred crime and reformed criminals. What I didn't know was what was going on inside. Now I know a lot more.

Many of the sentences don't fit the crime. I was startled—and still am—by how the actual crimes committed by some of the women I met were petty, yet their sentences were long and unjust. Yes, some women have committed violent crimes, and their sentences protect the public, if they are indeed violent. But violence remains a minority offense for women.

There should be better help on the outside for mothers who are in prison. Often, they're the sole caregivers for their children, and prison may mean the slow crumbling of their families as their sons and daughters are unsatisfactorily farmed out to friends, family, foster homes, or other sources of inferior care.

There's inadequate support in prisons to wean women away from drug and alcohol misuse and too little invested in teaching them employable skills. The system desperately lacks a range of educational opportunities, which, if properly funded, could help women rebuild their lives.

An example that comes to my mind is Kimee, a young woman from Midland, Texas, whom I met at Carswell. She was only twenty-eight years old, slight in build, with wispy blonde hair and a face already lined with the troubles of life. Kimee had four children and was divorced. She got married when she was nineteen years old because she was pregnant. She had two kids with her husband and two afterwards with a boyfriend. This boyfriend got her into drugs, namely crystal meth, four years ago, even though she had never done drugs a day in her life. "The first time I shot meth in my arm, I stayed away for five days straight. I loved it and used to constantly get high. The meth helped me keep my weight off," she told me. "When I couldn't get high, I felt like there were bugs crawling all over me."

Kimee went from using it to also selling it with her boyfriend. Although she was doing jail time for six months, she was thankful for being sent to prison because it forced her to get away from her boyfriend and get sober. Unfortunately, Kimee still craved meth and knew that when she went back to Midland, she'd slip right back into the deadly cycle. It was disappointing to me that the only drug rehab program at Carswell was for offenders who have sentences longer than six months.

The system desperately lacks a range of educational opportunities, which, if properly funded, could help women rebuild their lives. It just makes sense to train women in a profession where they can achieve a decent level of pay. Considering that many incarcerated women are single mothers and must be the sole support of their family once they are released, prison education is the only hope.

Sadly, the policies we currently follow in this country seem more intent on punishing offenders than rehabilitating them. More restorative, not so much retributive, justice is needed. Many formerly incarcerated persons return to neighborhoods. If we value safe neighborhoods, we should implement stronger rehabilitative strategies for people serving time in prison.

It seems a daunting task to improve prison conditions, but we can't just turn our backs and walk away from the women in prison. It's important to try to help them, even if the improvements are few and far between. Certainly even what may seem like a small improvement could make a big difference for even just one woman in prison.

These things—the things I now stand for—give me positive energy. They give me passion. They give me a reason to live. I feel happier and more fulfilled than I was during my record-breaking days.

Time moves on, and I don't have any regrets. There are always things that could have been better, but I don't look back much. I prefer to look forward. I continually find wonderful opportunities appearing at my door. I am sought out by journalists and different publications who want to interview me. But I've scaled back fulfilling many of these requests so that I can focus on basketball and improve where I need to improve. I continue to be asked to give my Take a Break message to people, schools, companies, and organizations across the country.

I'm optimistic that this journey of mine is nowhere close to ending unless God has another plan for me. I truly believe that I'm on the right track, one that includes helping people live better and healthier lives. I'm hopeful that I will achieve a great amount of success in whatever direction God leads me in.

There are times when I fall short of what He wants, but I keep Him close always. Life can feel awfully lonely from time to time if we forget God's promise that "I will be with you always." It is my faith in God that keeps me going. That faith is based on my belief in

God's ability to work things out together for our good, as Paul says in Romans 8:28. Yes, God has a way of pulling me and pushing me down paths I would never choose. But no matter what setback or adversity I meet along the way, I look to Him to sustain me in the midst of any trial. I know that all things—not just some things but all things—are working together for my good. And I can take on anything life sends my way because of my faith.

People have often asked me how I wish to be remembered.

I don't want to be remembered for the records I broke, the races I won, or the medals I lost. I want to be remembered for the very worst mistake I ever made and how I turned it into a life-affirming positive for the world. I want my children, when they grow up, to look at my life and see that I was remembered for all the right reasons . . . as someone who scaled many hurdles, and when the course of life got rough and the paths were dark, I set out to make a difference, did my best, and stayed on the right track.